I0423434

Reality is Spiritual

Volume 1

Dreams and the Spiritual World Integrating the Psychology of Jung and Swedenborg

Leon James, Ph.D.

God, Immortality and Theistic Psychology Series

REGENERATION
MEDIA
PUBLICATIONS
KAILUA

http://www.theisticpsychology.org

Also Available: Volume 2

Reality is Spiritual

Rational Theistic Self-Analysis (RTS)
For Achieving Wholeness
Here and in the Afterlife

Leon James, Ph.D.

Reality is Spiritual: Dreams and the Spiritual World: Jung and Swedenborg

All quotes in this book from the work of Jung and Swedenborg were taken from public domain versions made available on the Internet and downloaded freely.

This is the First Edition published in June 2016

Paperback
ISBN: zzz

Dedication

This book is dedicated to my longtime cyber friend and colleague

Abe Venter

*Dedicated Counseling Psychologist to needy children in South Africa
Long time student, practitioner, and follower of
Carl Rogers, Carl Jung, and Emanuel Swedenborg*

"Altruism is the experiencing of God."

~Abe Venter

Contents

Reality is Spiritual Volume 1

Dedication 4
Introduction 7
About This Book Volume 1 and Volume 2 7
Are We Immortal? 10
About The Author 18

Chapter 1 About Carl Jung (1875-1961) 27
Time Line of Jung's Life 29
Jung Talking About Freud 33
Freud's Atheism vs. Jung's Theism 33
Jung and Freud Meet 37
Freud's Blindness to the Unconscious 41
The Jung Selection 44
Freud's Untrustworthiness 45
Jung Discovers the Psychogenesis of Dementia 47
Jung Discovers the Relevance of the Unconscious 48
Jung: Sexuality Is Freud's God 49
Jung's Dream Foreshadows Break With Freud 52
From the New York Times About Jung 57
Jung Resources on the Web 62

Chapter 2 About Emanuel Swedenborg (1688-1772) 65
What Some Notables in History Have Said About Swedenborg 70
Swedenborg Describes His Divine Mission and Calling 76
Swedenborg Books and Resources on the Web 85

Chapter 3 Jung on Dreams and the Psychic World 88
The Spiritual Reality of the Psychic World 89
Wholeness Requires That We Are To Know Ourselves 101
Looking Through the Window to the Unconscious 104
Individuation Within Collectivity 112
Sexuality: Freud, Jung, and Swedenborg 116
Dreams and Psychic Health 122
Religion vs. Creed 124
Dreams Possess Collective Meaning 125
The Art of Interpreting Dreams 129
We Do Not Produce Dreams: They Come To Us 138
Sacred Scripture or the Word of God 147
Archetypes and Psychology 150
Religion and Myth 153
The Symbolism of Water 155

Chapter 4 Swedenborg on Dreams and the Spiritual World 162
Consciousness When Dreaming 169
Vertical and Horizontal Consciousness 170
Swedenborg's Correspondences and Jung's Archetypes 179
How And By Whom Dreams Are Produced 188
Visions 212

God, Immortality and Theistic Psychology Series by Dr. Leon James 215

Introduction

About This Book
Volume 1 and Volume 2

If a man knows more than others, he becomes lonely.
~Carl Jung, Memories, Dreams, Reflections, 1962

The Word is the only doctrine which teaches how a man
must live in the world in order to be happy to eternity.
~Swedenborg, Arcana Coelestia, AC 8939

For us humans, once alive, always alive. You are now in
the natural phase of your eternity. The three-day dying-
resuscitation procedure ends that phase and begins the
spiritual phase of immortality. ~Leon James

Carl Jung   Emanuel Swedenborg   Leon James

The ideas of Carl Jung (1875-1961) and Emanuel Swedenborg (1688-1772) have brought to psychology a whole new direction that gives people the ability to think about themselves as immortal spiritual beings.

Thanks to these two giants of psychology people today are receiving knowledge about the spiritual reality in which they are born and in which they live forever. *Reality is spiritual.* Everything in the universe was created by God so that it may serve and be useful to the human race.

No thing exists that does not in some way contribute to the goal of human existence and life.

This is a human universe.

Why then does reality seem so cold, so materialistic, so dark and inhuman? I will use the ideas of Jung and Swedenborg to show that this constricted and unhappy view of reality is a <u>false appearance</u> that we perceive and experience when we blind ourselves to the spiritual depth that lies within the human mind of every individual.

Jung looked within his mind and discovered through the *process of experiencing* the larger world that exists *within* the human psyche. He allowed his inner senses to be awakened from their slumber and then he could perceive the unfathomable vastness and darkness of the collective unconscious, which is what binds together all human minds, past, present, and future.

My thesis, then, is as follows: In addition to our immediate consciousness, which is of a thoroughly personal nature and which we believe to be the only empirical psyche (even if we tack on the personal unconscious as an appendix), there exists a second psychic system of a collective, universal, and impersonal nature which is identical in all individuals. ~Carl Jung, The Archetypes and the Collective Unconscious, 1936, p. 43

The real Self of every human being lies in that vast mental universe of eternity, apart from time, apart from space, and not subject to the limits of physical matter. Jung taught that to be psychologically healthy and whole, or self-realized and individuated, every person must go on the spiritual hunt to track the Self down in that vast and murky psychic universe.

It is a scary experience to make this discovery by which we become exposed to the raw and awesome psychic forces that exist in our unconscious mind.

Readers of Jung have discovered this same mental reality in their own experiencing of the depth that lies within the mind of every person.

By looking inward we too can discover the same things that Jung discovered and wrote about. It is human to want to know our present and our future reality.

I have now seen quite a number of people die in the time of a great transition, reaching as it were the end of their pilgrimage in sight of the Gates, where the way bifurcates to the land of Hereafter and to the future of mankind and its spiritual adventure. You had a glimpse of the Mysterium Magnum.
~Carl Jung, Letters Vol. II, p. 604

If ever you have the rare opportunity to speak with the devil, then do not forget to confront him in all seriousness. He is your devil after all. ~Carl Jung, Liber Novus, p. 261

Whoever lives and believes in Me, shall never die. ~Jesus, New Testament, John xi 25, 26

*Our eternal destiny is in our
power through the choices
we make in daily life. ~Leon
James*

Death is a drawing together of two worlds, not an
end. We are the bridge. ~Carl Jung, J.E.T., p. 95

Are We Immortal?

We certainly want to be! What is it like to live in the afterlife? What are
the afterlife lifestyles? Can we see God? *How are we to prepare
ourselves now for that life in eternity?* I answer these critical questions in
my book *Experiencing Regeneration: Equipping Our Personality For
Living In The Afterlife* (2015) (Print and Kindle versions at Amazon.com).

In the following pages I will present the definitive answers and
explanations given by Jung and Swedenborg on the question of our
immortality.

How do we live a spiritual life while we are in a natural world and body?
Is this even possible? What is a spiritual life?

In every generation there are people who might be called "seekers" or
"seekers of truth". People long for a spiritual consciousness and all sorts
of schools and methods exist to assist those who seek spiritual truth.

Spiritual truths are ideas that can rationally answer such questions as
the following: What is the most important task we have here on earth? If
there is life after death in eternity then why are we born on earth instead
of in eternity? Do we have a soulmate with whom we live in happiness to
eternity? Is there marriage in the afterlife? What is our spiritual body like
and can we feel and do the same things as in the physical body? What

is love? What is truth? How does God relate to each individual personally?

And furthermore: Can we meet the people who already live in the afterlife? Are there spirits and angels? Is there a devil? How do we equip our personality with traits of mutual love that allows us to be angels in eternity? How do we avoid becoming selfish and stupid, unhappy and non-productive, living below the level of our human potential?

And finally: Ho do we achieve self-realization and spiritual enlightenment?

Every one of these questions will be answered in this book. Furthermore, the answers are presented as rational explanations based on the empirical observations and vast research compiled by the two giants of psychology, Jung and Swedenborg. In most cases these are answers that can be found elsewhere echoed in pieces and scattered across the world literature of the past three thousand years. The unparalleled genius and knowledge of Jung and Swedenborg provide the basis for presenting a coherent rational and unified scientific theory of the immortal human mind and of God's very close relationship to the human race and to every individual.

More than anyone in history and science Swedenborg has brought to people a definite and specific knowledge of the dying process, the resuscitation after death into the afterlife world of eternity, and *the detailed ethnographic descriptions of lifestyles in the afterlife*, including the landscapes, the people, psychic cities, and habitations of heaven and hell, which are not places but good and bad mental states in every person's mind.

These two together, Jung and Swedenborg, are giants in the history of psychology who enrich our knowledge and imagination of our present and of our immortal future. This book collects their ideas into short quotations and longer selections of what they wrote about the psychic world, God, death, immortality, resurrection, love, dreams, and other vibrant ideas from depth psychology, analytical psychology, and theistic psychology. The author, Leon James, who is knowledgeable in theistic psychology, shows how the ideas of Jung and Swedenborg complement each other, enriching our understanding of the spiritual topics they

11

discuss and have become so vital to our modern technological generation.

A fundamental issue in Jungian psychology is the balance that needs to be achieved by every individual between two universal archetypes that exist in our collective unconscious. These are named the *animus*, for the masculine aspect of human beings, and the *anima*, for their feminine aspect. Every person must have both aspects integrated in their psyche in order to be mentally wholesome and productive. This important anatomical principle in Jung is closely related to Swedenborg's anatomical principle by which our will (or volition) and our understanding (or meaning) together form the basis of all mental functioning in every individual. The *will* is the organ responsible for the act of willing things in everyone, and includes what is affective, emotional, intuitive, definitive, passionate, and clinging to conjunction with another person and with God.

Thus, the will may be called the anima or feminine aspect of every individual's personality.

The will has a companion or conjugal partner that is called our understanding. It is the cognitive function in our thinking, reasoning, imagining, and planning. Anatomically viewed relative to the will, the understanding is like the outside relative to the inside. In every object there is an outside and an inside, as in fruit, wood, stone, box, wall, kidney, heart, and so on. No object of use exists that does not have an outside and an inside. For the object to continue to exist the outside and the inside must conjoin and work together. In Swedenborg's work this conjunction in human minds is called *the spiritual marriage*. It is the marriage between our will and our understanding, a conjunction that makes possible all sensation and motor activity in the spiritual body and in the physical body.

Anatomically viewed, the human mind is made of mental or spiritual organs, or organic components, that are arranged in a series of fibrous layers on top of one another. Each anatomical layer has an outside and an inside. The "higher" layers may also be conceptualized as the "inner" layers. In anatomy as in physics the inner layers of something are higher and more complex than its outer layers. The human mind is also called the mental world, or the psychic world, or the spiritual world. The unconscious layer of an individual's mind overlaps, or is the same as, the collective unconscious. Through human biology we all have the same unconscious psychic layers, hence the name "collective" unconscious.

The quality of the spiritual marriage of the will and the understanding in an individual is the fundamental issue for spiritual self-analysis. In other words, the way the affective system (anima) and the cognitive system (animus) work together determines our mental health, our spirituality, and our consciousness.

Both Jung and Swedenborg talk about this principle of human anatomical functioning, but in different terms that yet are compatible and mutually enrich each other in meaning. The marriage of the animus and the anima *within each mind* is the fundamental issue for the mental health of the person. Jung observed that men tend to resist this marriage within their personality.

Jung observed that men fear their female aspect (affective) as a threat to their masculinity and potency (cognitive). Women on the other hand embrace their animus or masculine element in their mind, allowing it to conjoin in their personality with their anima. This allows women's passion, feelings, and love (affective) to be influenced by their intellect and reasoning (cognitive). Women allow their affective (feeling) and cognitive (thinking) systems to accommodate to each other in their mind and to form a stable union in functioning.

Nevertheless men have no choice, according to Jung and Swedenborg, but to undergo this spiritual marriage within themselves between their masculine-cognitive and feminine-affective spiritual aspects. Prior to this inner marriage within oneself men do not understand women, nor really like them. This may be the basis for why men have mistreated and belittled women throughout history and why they still do that today.

In natural consciousness, prior to progress in regeneration or individuation, gender is identified primarily by the physical body and secondarily by the mentality and its personality. But later in the path to self-realization and regeneration, gender is primarily identified with mentality and personality, and secondarily with the physical body.

While they are still immersed in material or natural consciousness, without as yet an active spirituality, men may feel a deep-seated inner antipathy for women of which they are not fully conscious. This spontaneous and involuntary dislike is not visibly displayed except at certain times of challenge or conflict in the relationship, at which time men become insulting to women, abusive, and violent, revealing the antipathy and even hatred of women that lies buried in their personality. This negative and anti-feminine behavior and intentionality by men reveals the deep-seated dislike and hatred that men have of women. The dislike of women by men leads them to abuse women, which is done in all cultures.

At the same time, men want women around for the rewards that they provide to men such as sex, offspring, domestic work, and extra income. When it comes to companionship, the majority of single men and husbands pick male friends to be with, to relax, and to have fun with. Men secretly consider women as second-class citizens and incomplete human beings in comparison to men. In many countries and cultures men can legally abuse women and restrict their human rights, including forcing them to marry as children, to wear uncomfortable and unattractive clothes, and to ask a man's permission (parent, brother, uncle) when making important social decisions. This is the order of the natural consciousness of a man's animus that has not yet been conjoined to his inner anima.

> Jung told a man to spend an hour a day by himself, to find what he was inside. "But then I would get quite melancholy, "the man replied. "Exactly," said Jung, "It is very depressing to be by yourself. But how do you think I can stand you? It is a test to stand yourself. If you can stand yourself, then the world might be able to stand you, but certainly nobody can stand you otherwise. It is like someone who is unwashed."
> ~Carl Jung, Visions Seminar, p. 369

Progress in personality development or individuation is possible only when we allow our spiritual consciousness to enlighten the natural consciousness and thereby give it a higher order of functioning.

Jung said that to look outside is to be blind, but to look inside is to see. And also, that to analyze one's dreams is to wake up.

This book reviews the meaning and psychodynamics of symbolism in dreams and in the unconscious as found in the work of Jung and Swedenborg. Swedenborg's theistic psychology clarifies the spiritual symbolism that is hidden in *Sacred Scripture* in its more interior layer, and what critical role these Divine "correspondences" play in our psychological development and growth.

This book is not about professional Jungian therapy or spiritual counseling. The author Leon James is not a Jungian analyst or psychiatrist and has never been a therapist. Thousands of people are reading Jung's books and deriving benefits in thinking about themselves and understanding the world. Being a trained analyst and counselor is one possible approach to Jung's ideas and principles. Another approach is to read Jung's pages and try to apply their contents to oneself. This involves various areas of focus of the personality such as understanding the psychodynamic symbolism and power of dreams, understanding God and our relationship to God, and discovering the awesomeness of the collective unconscious and how our individual ego is connected to it or is immersed in it.

This is what I have done, reading Jung's collected works available on the Internet and various contemporary commentaries and current blogs on the Web that are concerned with Jung's ideas today. Studying Swedenborg has been a longtime intellectual passion of mine, so it makes sense that when I started studying Jung I interconnected the ideas of Jung and Swedenborg and came to see how they enriched and clarified each other.

I realized that the two authors together provide a deeper understanding of each alone. That is what motivated me to write this book and share that insight.

Jung's writings, lectures, letters, and interviews are all available on the Web. Never before have so many people gotten involved in his ideas. In this book I focus on a highly significant statement Jung made about himself, which was that God was the center of focus and interest all his life. This is a little known fact, especially because of the way Jung talked about God in his published writings. Still today, some "Jungians" or readers of Jung see Jung's involvement with God as an interest in archetypes and comparative religions. They do not acknowledge that Jung had a personal relationship with God on a significant basis.

In this book I present evidence that clearly shows Jung's central relationship to God that spanned from his childhood days to the last months of his life in this world. I also focus on Jung's great spiritual discovery that he called "the collective unconscious". This may be the most imprtant and most exciting discovery in psychology in the 20th century. Through Jung's work scientific dualism was introduced in modern science.   Perhaps not everyone is fully aware of the fact that the collective unconscious does not exist in the physical world. It exists in the psychic world, which is independent of the physical world and exists apart from space and apart from time. This is known in science as "dualism".

Science and technology have indeed conquered the world, but whether the psyche has gained anything is another matter. ~Carl Jung, CW 13, Para 163

Freud and the rest of the prominent scientists of the 20th century rejected and ridiculed the idea of two worlds. To Freud the psychic "world" was not a real world like the natural world is a real world. Freud was a materialist, a monist, an opponent of dualism. Psyche, soul, ego, pdychodynamic forces, self, ego, consciousness – these for Freud were not real objects since they were psychological or mental, and those are not real. To realize this is quite shocking about Freud since this view renders all of Freudian psychology merely a mechanical metaphor, not psychological reality. I present some views on Freud that Jung shared in an interview and in some of his articles. Jung said that Freud had no genuine understanding of dream analysis because his rigid materialism and passionate atheism put up a block to the reality of the psyche and psychic world.

Jung's discovery of the psychic world as independent reality was only the second time in the history of psychology that the perspective of scientific dualism was presented. The first time was about one hundred years before Jung's birth when Swedenborg publsihed his Writings on the ethnography of the psychic world.

Soul and body are not two things. They are one.
~Carl Jung, Zarathustra Seminar, p. 355

Every person consists of three components which follow in order in him: soul, mind, and body. The inmost one is his soul. The intermediate one is his mind. And the outmost one is his body. Everything that flows into a person from the Lord flows first into his inmost component, which is the soul, and descends from there into his intermediate component, which is the mind, and through this into his outmost component, which is the body.

A marriage of good and truth flows in from the Lord in a person in the same way. It flows into his soul directly, and continues from there into the subsequent faculties, and through these to the outmost constituents. And thus conjointly they bring about conjugial love. It is apparent from a consideration of this influx that a married couple is an image of the marriage between good and truth in their inmost qualities and thus in their subsequent ones.
~Swedenborg, Conjugial Love, CL 101

About The Author

Dr. Leon James has been Professor of Psychology at the University Hawaii since 1971. He has also held academic positions at McGill University, Laval University, University of Wisconsin, and University of Illinois. Since 1960 he has conducted research, published articles and books, and taught courses in several scientific specialty subjects that include the following:

social-personality theory and measurement; statistics and research design; psycholinguistics and ethnosemantics; ethnomethodology and intersubjectivity; discourse analysis; language learning and teaching; library and information science; driving psychology; road rage; sidewalk rage; air rage; the spiritual psychology of Emanuel Swedenborg; theistic psychology; cyberpsychology; marriage and couplehood.

Dr. James is the Editor-in-Chief of the *Journal of Psychology and Clinical Psychiatry*, and he is on the Editorial Board of various academic journals including *Acta Psychopathologica Journal*. He regularly consults with safety organizations and institutions worldwide on driving psychology. He is considered an expert on "road rage", "air rage" and "sidewalk rage", and has given well over one thousand newspaper interviews and media appearances. In 1997 he was among the first to give expert testimony to the Transportation Sub-Committee of the U.S. Congress on the then emerging topic of road rage and aggressive driving. Since then road rage and aggressive driving have continued to increase, killing thousands of victims every year and injuring millions of people yearly. His book with Diane Nahl *Road Rage and Aggressive Driving* (2000) provides behavioral methods to help drivers gain control over their traffic emotions. These methods have been taught to thousands of people throughout the United States who are preparing to obtain a driver's license.

In fifty years of scientific research and writing Leon James introduced more than two thousand *neologisms* or novel expressions that refer to new scientific ideas that he discovered or invented. Some of these expressions have been picked up by others and are in use today. The oldest and most successful of his neologisms is the expression "*semantic satiation*" which was the topic of his Masters Thesis and Ph.D. Dissertation at McGill University in 1962. Semantic satiation refers to the change or loss of meaning of a word when it is repeated beyond a certain frequency (see Wikipedia article). He demonstrated how this neuro-semantic phenomenon applies to various situations, including vocabulary learning, doing simple arithmetic, enjoyment of popular songs, stuttering on the phone, bilingualism, remembering TV commercials, and focusing on visual displays. In the past few years semantic satiation has been researched in dozens of articles in psychology, instruction, business, art, music, and aesthetics. It has now become a popular topic of chat discussions and a name for blogs, chat rooms, bands, albums, and videos. Semantic satiation is also entering the common vocabulary of people in their everyday use.

Another of his neologisms that entered into popular use is the expression "*road rage nursery*" to refer to the back seat of a car. This was meant to alert parents that the way they verbalize and behave behind the wheel in traffic will function as a model for the children in the back seat when they grow up and start driving on their own. Another expression he coined that became popular in the language-teaching field is "*communicative competence*". This idea was meant to make a distinction between mere linguistic competence and the actual ability to use the language for communication. Since then this distinction and term has become of standard use in the field of language teaching and testing.

However most of his neologisms remained unaddressed by others. Some of these are: "*cross-modality transfer effect*", "*ethnosemantic*

19

hexagram series" (viz.: trigram, hexagram, ennead, double hexagram, electric couple), "*existential neologisms*", "*mental anatomy*", "*the mental world of eternity*", "*vertical community*", and "*self-witnessing*". The full list of his neologisms with explanations is available on the Web at: http://theisticpsychology.org/books/neologisms/neochartp1.htm

For the past thirty years he has focused his research especially on the *Writings of Swedenborg*, looking for ways to transform Swedenborg's spiritual reports and ideas into the language and theory of modern scientific psychology. Leon James coined the expression "theistic psychology" in 1990. He acknowledges that Emanuel Swedenborg (1688-1772) is the actual founder of theistic psychology, even though Swedenborg himself did not use this expression. This book is the latest instance of that continuing task of bringing Swedenborg's ideas to the science of psychology and the practice of self-analysis.

Several striking spiritual explanations emerge from this effort. Here I will just mention the following four vitally important new ideas to which I was led by studying the Swedenborg Reports.

(a) Born Immortal

A central idea is the novel principle, which is unheard of in modern psychology, that *the spiritual world of the afterlife is the mental world of eternity*. In other words, we are born into mental eternity.

This may be the greatest discovery of my career. The consequence of this equation is that *every human being is born into eternity and thereby is immortal*.

At "death" we do not have to "pass into" the spiritual world of the afterlife since we are born into it and never leave it. There is no mental activity possible in the physical brain or world. Hence our mind and personality are born and develop in that mental world that is shared in common by all human beings. After we awaken from the three-day dying-resuscitation procedure we are fully conscious in the afterlife world and are then able to see and socialize with all those who have preceded us there.

Every mind and its personality or self is immortal because it already exists in eternity. Therefore in this book instead of discussing "death" I discuss the "three-day dying-resuscitation procedure" by which our spiritual body is disjoined from the inert physical body. We then immediately gain consciousness of the surrounds and begin to interact with the people who are already living in the afterlife. Our spiritual body upon resuscitation has the same appearance as our former physical body, but this changes after a little while.

In short: afterlife of eternity = spiritual world = mental world of eternity.

This leads to the following astonishing three-part conclusion and spiritual realization:

(a) We are born immortal.
(b) Our mind, personality, thoughts and feelings are already now in the afterlife of eternity.
(c) Everyone is in the same mental world of eternity, and hence every human being has access to every other human being past and present.

The above are facts discovered and confirmed by Swedenborg through his unique capability of making observations in dual consciousness.

(b) Vertical Community

A second striking insight from Swedenborg needed a new name to express the idea in the language of modern psychology, namely, the existence of the *vertical community*. This idea describes how every individual's mental life is anatomically connected to the mental life of those who are already in the afterlife. *There is therefore a hitherto unknown anatomical interconnection from each human being to every other*. This amazing new view expands the meaning of community from "horizontal community" that depends on geographical place and time, to "vertical community" that is independent of fixed time and place.

The psychological implications of this discovery are numerous and remain to be followed up. The concept of a vertical community opens up whole new areas of study, research, and application in human mental health and in community organization.

Swedenborg confirmed the above fact by repeated experiments and interviews of those who are in the afterlife of eternity, which he called the "spiritual world". From age 57 to 83 Swedenborg was conscious in both this world, as we are, and also of the world of the afterlife, as we also are but only after death. In this state of uninterrupted dual consciousness for 27 years he was able to write a careful ethnography of the vertical community and how they impact on human consciousness and personality.

(c) As-of Self (Instead of Self)

The third new idea I translated for modern psychology is the idea of the *as-of self*.

This concept proposes the next phase of human evolution regarding ego and personality. When we think of ourselves as an "as-of self" we are able to overcome the illusion that our mental life is from ourselves. This illusion ignores the actuality of the vertical community, and this results in many debilitating symptoms in psychological functioning and interpersonal relations. Equally important, the "as-of self" concept clarifies the relationship between individual freedom and God's omnipotence.

Experiencing regeneration is possible with the "as-of self" concept because it allows us to separate ourselves from selfish loves and inherited evil inclinations. *Psychologically we can now stop identifying with negative feelings and intentions*, and this gives us the freedom and opportunity to adopt new altruistic traits. This process equips our personality with positive traits that will allow us to enjoy the life of heaven in the afterlife.

This spiritual idea of the self or ego clarifies two big puzzles in the literature of theology and transpersonal psychology. On the one hand, we are free individual agents and therefore responsible for our deeds and attitudes. On the other hand, God is omnipotent which logically means that we have no real freedom. If that's the case, then (a) why does God allow evil to exist, and (b) why do we end up in hell for leading a selfish and evil life when we had no real freedom.

The as-of self is a psychological and rational solution to all these difficult issues. See my articles on the theisticpsychology.org web site. More on this concept is reviewed in this book.

(d) Mental Anatomy

The fourth concept I wish to mention here is the idea that *mind has an anatomy and organic structure*. Without functioning organs, the mind cannot be real. Hence arose materialism and reductionism in materialistic psychology whereby the mind is tied completely to the physical brain and not actually existing in its own realm, world, or substantive permanence. In the current "modern" materialistic view, when the brain dies, so does the mind. This idea is disturbing to people because it gives them the idea of being impermanent, and this is the experiencing of death rather than continuation of life.

Everything in psychology changes when one considers my new proposal of *mental anatomy*, which restores scientific dualism to historical psychology. Now for the first time, the psychology of mind and consciousness is discussed as *anatomy of the spiritual body* and its threefold system called affective, cognitive, and sensorimotor. This means that everyone is born into two worlds simultaneously with a temporary physical body that is functionally connected to a permanent spiritual body that houses our ego, self, personality, thoughts, and feelings. At death the physical body is functionally detached from the spiritual body, and this separation does not affect the self or mind in any way.

Swedenborg spent 27 continuous years living and exploring the afterlife world of eternity at the same time that he maintained a busy and successful career as a mining engineer, publisher of scientific journals, and active participant in legislation in the Swedish House of Lords.

Denying God leads to love of oneself, and this is a ticket to hell. Visual proof for this is provided by Swedenborg. ~Leon James

Dr. Leon James started studying *Swedenborg's Writings* in 1981. Full text and free access to most of his theistic psychology books and articles is available at the Theistic Psychology Web Site http://theisticpsychology.org/index.htm managed by Dr. Ian Thompson, author of *Starting Science from God: Rational Scientific Theories from Theism*.

Truth is visible to awareness while its love is hidden within it. ~Leon James

All my doubts are so many sins against God. ~Leon James

If truth is the chair, then love is its wood.
If love is the flower, then truth is its stalk.
If truth is water, love is its steam.
If love is heat, truth is its light.
~Leon James

Insight is foresight.
~Leon James

Consciousness is the awareness of experiencing. Therefore such as is the quality of awareness such is the consciousness. Experiencing is what happens. There is no other venue for anything to happen. ~Leon James

The immortality of the person is nothing else than the flow of experiencing that cannot cease. ~Leon James

To love others as much as loving oneself, and God above all is the experiencing of spiritual consciousness. . ~Leon James

A husband loves what he understands. A wife understands what she loves. ~Leon James

In order to understand himself, a spiritual husband relies on his wife. ~Leon James

Anatomically viewed, a husband and a wife together make up one complete human being. The conjoined pair is the complete person. She is his heart and he is her lungs. ~Leon James

Consciousness is omnipresent. God is omnipresent.
Consciousness is human. God is Human.
God creates human beings to be reception organs for consciousness.
An individual's consciousness is unique, human, immortal, and omnipresent.
We receive God's inflowing consciousness at three levels of perfection in our mind: celestial-rational, spiritual-rational, and spiritual-natural.
~Leon James

*To be in the highest heaven in eternity is to experience **celestial**-rational consciousness. Here we love others more than self for the sake of good.*
*To be in the middle heaven in eternity is to experience **spiritual**-rational consciousness. Here we love others more than self for the sake of truth.*
*To be in the lower heaven in eternity is to experience spiritual-**natural** consciousness. Here we love others as much as self for the sake of conscience.*
~Leon James

There are three things in a man that a woman wants more than all other things—friendship, cooperation, and wisdom.

A wife wants friendship from her husband because she needs to feel stimulated and free. These are the feelings that come from being the best of friends. This includes intimacy and sexuality as an eternal couple.

A wife wants cooperation from her husband because her life is miserable and hard when he resists her in this or that, following his own mind.

A wife wants wisdom in her husband so that she could admire him and feel safe and protected from false perspectives and dangerous involvements which otherwise she might fall prey to. ~Leon James

END OF INTRODUCTION

Chapter 1
About Carl Jung
(1875-1961)

Where is a height without depth, and how can there be light that throws no shadow? There is no good that is not opposed by evil. ~Carl Jung, CW 10, Para 271

"I don't believe. I know."

Whether he understands them or not, man must remain conscious of the world of the archetypes, because in it he is still a part of nature and is connected to his own roots.
~Carl Jung, Symbols of Transformation, p. 23

You cannot get out of your skin until you become an eternal ghost.
~Carl Jung, 1925 Seminar, p. 79

Why do I have to talk about God? Because He is everywhere! I am only the spoon in His kitchen.
~Carl Jung, J.E.T., p. 109

From the beginning I had a sense of destiny, as though my life was assigned to me by fate and had to be fulfilled. This gave me an inner security, and, though I could never prove it to myself, it proved itself to me. I did not have this certainty, it had me. ~Carl Jung, Memories, Dreams, Reflections, p.48

Occultist, Scientist, Prophet, Charlatan – C. G. Jung has been called all these things and after decades of myth making is one of the most misunderstood figures in Western intellectual history. ~Sonu Shamdasani, Jung and the Making of Modern Psychology: The Dream of a Science, 2004

Carl Gustav Jung (1875-1961) was a well-known Swiss psychiatrist and founder of analytical psychology. He made significant contributions in psychiatry, psychology, anthropology, and religious studies. He was a prolific writer throughout his long career and some of his books were only published posthumously. He was a world traveller and gave many interviews and lectures that were well received. He carried out a voluminous correspondence with various people and most of these were published after his death. Today there are millions of people who study Jung's works and practice Jungian counseling, depth psychology therapy, and self-realization efforts.

Just as a man brings forth his work as a complete creation out of his inner feminine nature, so the inner masculine side of a woman brings forth creative seeds which have the power to fertilize the feminine side of the man. ~Carl Jung, CW 7, Para 336

Time Cover Story, 1955

Time Line of Jung's Life

1875 Born in Kesswil, Switzerland
1879 Moved to Basel
1895 Student at University of Basel
1900 Graduated from Basel
1900 Assistant physician under Eugen Bleuler
1902 Obtained M.D. from University of Zurich
1902 Went to Paris and heard Pierre Janet
1902 Went to London
1903 Married Emma Rauschenbach
1904 Research in Word Association
1905 Started lecturing at Zurich
1907 First meeting with Sigmund Freud
1909 Gave up work at Burgholzi

1911 Lectured in the United States with Freud
1911 Elected president of the "International Psychoanalytic Society"
1912 Publication of "Psychology of the Unconscious"
1912 Split with Freud
1913 Gave up lectureship at Zurich
1914 Resigned from the "International Psychoanalytic Society"
1920 Went to Tunis and Algiers
1921 Publication of "Psychological Types"
1924 Studied Pueblo Indians
1926 Studied the inhabitants of Mount Elgon in Kenya
1933 Professor of Psychology at the Federal Polytechnical University of Zurich
1933 Edited the "Central Journal for Self-analysis and Related Fields"
1935 President of the Swiss Society for Practical Psychology
1937 Visited India
1939 Finished editing the "Central Journal for Self-analysis and Related Fields"
1941 Retired from The Federal Polytechnical University of Zurich
1943 Professor of Medical Psychology at the University of Basel
1961 Died in Kusnacht, on Lake Zurich

As a child I felt myself to be alone, and I am still, because I know things and must hint at things which others apparently know nothing of, and for the most part do not want to know.
~ C.G. Jung, Memories, Dreams, Reflections

I am alone, but I fill my solitariness with my life.
~Carl Jung, Liber Novus, p. 277

The central concept of analytical psychology is individuation—the psychological process of integrating the opposites, including the conscious with the unconscious, while still maintaining their relative autonomy. Jung considered individuation to be the central process of human development.

Jung's best known concepts include the archetype, the collective unconscious, psychological complexes, extraversion, and introversion.

Of prime importance to Jung was the detailing of the stages of inner development and of the growth of the personality, which he termed the "process of individuation." He described a strong impulse from the unconscious to guide the individual toward its most complete uniqueness. This achievement is a lifelong task of trial and error and identifying and uniting contents of the unconscious. It consists in an ever-increasing self-knowledge and in "becoming what you are."

Jung lived for his explorations, his writings, and his psychological practice, which he had to give up in 1944 due to a severe heart attack. His career included the professorship of medical psychology at the University of Basel and the titular (title without the actual position) professorship of philosophy from 1933 until 1942 on the faculty of philosophical and political sciences of the Federal Institute of Technology in Zurich. In 1948 he founded the C. G. Jung Institute in Zurich. Honorary doctorates were given to him by many important universities all over the world.

Carl Jung was a prolific letter writer. Much of Jung's writings can be very difficult reading, particularly when he digs deep into complex subjects like alchemy. But his letters are often poetic and

reveal his humanity and his passionate engagement with the struggles of living an authentic and meaningful life.
~Jason E. Smith, Jungian Psychoanalyst

Carl Jung was among the deepest philosophical thinkers of the modern era. He examined many aspects of the self, trying to better understand the human experience. Jung thought we were all spiritual beings, not simply a flesh and blood vessel experiencing the universe for no reason. From: Higher Perspective Web Site

He [Jung] felt the need to represent his innermost thoughts in stone and to build a completely primitive dwelling: "Bollingen was a great matter for me, because words and paper were not real enough. I had to put down a confession in stone." ~Sonu Shamdasani, Introduction 1925 Seminar, Page xiii

The tower [Jung's] was a "representation of individuation." Over the years, he painted murals and made carvings on the walls. The tower [Jung's] may be regarded as a three-dimensional continuation of Liber Novus: its "Liber Quartus." ~Sonu Shamdasani, Introduction 1925 Seminar, p. xiii

The Freudian idea that religion is nothing more than a system of prohibitions is very limited and out of touch with what is known about different religions. ~Carl Jung, Letters Vol. II, p. 631-632

Jung Talking About Freud

Our natural model is Christ. We have stood under his law since antiquity; first outwardly, and then inwardly. At first we knew this, and then knew it no longer. We fought against Christ, we deposed him, and we seemed to be conquerors. But he remained in us and mastered us. ~Carl Jung, Liber Novus, p. 293

Freud's Atheism vs. Jung's Theism

At the end of this Section I present a long Selection from Jung talking about his relationship to Freud. The following is my discussion and interpretation of the Jung Selection. I believe my discussion may be helpful to readers as an introduction and context to appreciate more fully the Jung Selection. However, if you rather read the selection first, you can, and then you may want to come back here for my discussion.

I am glad that Jung lectured about Freud intending to bring light to their famous relationship. The Selection discusses the personal and intellectual contrast between these two historical figures. Freud and Jung in retrospect have turned out to be two key figures for the future of psychology. Today millions of people are adopting their way of thinking and talking about human beings and about themselves as individuals.

These two intellectual innovators and popular leaders offer two distinct and radically opposed psychologies.

Freud, the passionate atheist, and Jung the dedicated theist, present opposite views on the self and the world. Freud ridiculed his patients for their *"childish dependency on a father figure"*, namely God. He wrote scholarly works about religion and history through the lens of the atheist to whom Sacred Scriptures in all cultures are merely myth and legend, thus psychologically motivated *fantasies*. Freud represents an important segment of twentieth-century intellectualism and his ideas and interpretations fit in with a lot of scholarly and literary activity. Many would prefer to characterize Freud as a "materialist" and "scientific positivist" rather than an atheist, which they would view as a biographical personal detail which, they argue, may not be relevant to the issue of Freud's position in history and psychology.

However to me it is clear that the characterization of atheism is central to understanding Freud's work and his continued influence in psychology and psychiatry. Freud's atheism is also central to understanding the difference and contrast between Freud and Jung.

Jung's theism pervades and suffuses all his work and life.

Jung himself could not have put it more pointedly when he declared near the end of his life on earth that God had been at the center of his life since childhood. This focus on God was personal, but not merely personal. *Jung made God a part of his psychology and his most central concepts.* God was everywhere in the human mind, active, determinative, involved, sometimes harsh and scary like a stern father, sometimes irresistibly attractive and loving. This is true theism in science.

Jung's psychology does not exist without God.

This assertion may be disputed by many Jungians today. I am reminded of what Jung is supposed to have said to Campbell: "*I am glad I am Jung, not a Jungian.*" I have a feeling that Jung may have been referring to his personal and intimate relationship with God that he maintained all his life since early childhood and never wavered or left behind, in contrast to his many of colleagues and fellow-scientists. Jung did not directly reveal this relationship in his writings until a few months before his death when he was dictating his memoirs for his last work, a book he insisted must be published only after his death. Jung hinted at the centrality of God in his life, which however he camouflaged by frequently using the expression "the God" and "the God-image" and "the Christ archetype".

I can see from this Jungian vocabulary usage how Jungians who are not committed to theism may conclude that by "God" Jung did not really mean God, but as a natural psychic force in the human mind. I expect most Jungian reading this book would be surprised at my insistence that Jung meant God in the normal sense and that God was the central beam throughout his long life on earth.

> *Keep it far from me, science that clever knower, that bad prison master who binds the soul and imprisons it in a lightless cell.*
> *~Carl Jung, The Red Book, p. 238*
>
> *But just as Judas is a necessary link in the chain of the work of redemption, so is our Judas betrayal of the hero also a necessary passageway to redemption. ~Carl Jung, Liber Novus, p. 242*
>
> *You serve the spirit of this time, and believe that you are able to escape the spirit of the depths. But the depths do not hesitate any longer and will force you into the mysteries of Christ. ~Carl Jung, Liber Novus, p. 253*
>
> *To be Christ oneself is the true following of Christ. ~Carl Jung, Liber Novus, p. 254*

If one accepts Jung's references to God as meant literally, one can clearly see in Jung's works that he did not merely talk about God personally. Jung did not merely acknowledge his unwavering religious faith as being the source of his life journey and psychic adventures and awesome discoveries. *Jung did the unthinkable in his medical profession: he brought God directly into science.* Jung made God a scientific concept in psychology. Once you think of God as pre-eminent and active in every individual's mind from birth onward, which is theism, it is impossible to exclude God from psychology and self-analysis.

The new scientific way of thinking about human beings that we associate with modern psychology came into existence in the 17th and 18th centuries. Since then psychology has maintained a central focus on change and growth in the individual and the group – personality development, social communication, and self-directed behavioral management.

Jung was a longtime psychiatrist by profession and in his lectures, letters, and writings he frequently discusses the personality problems of his many patients, attempting to illustrate empirically the existence of particular psychic phenomena acting in the mind of the patient. Both Freud and Jung saw themselves as scientists practicing a scientific approach to psychology and medicine. Early in his career during the period he was associated with Freud, Jung came to fundamentally reject Freud's work on neuroses and dream interpretation. Jung concluded after various interactions with Freud that he could not walk in the same steps as Freud, whom he found intellectually dishonest, as for instance Freud's policy to let mistakes stand in prior articles or decisions, on the principle that correcting things would weaken the authority of the profession. Still others are mentioned by Jung in the long Selection below.

Legitimate" faith must always rest on experience.
~Carl Jung, CW 5, Para 345

You may have, say, a religious attitude, which means an attitude of great totality, so that you receive the next leaf that falls from the tree as a message from God, and it works. ~Carl Jung, Visions Seminar, p. 919

It is only in modern times that the dream, this fleeting and insignificant-looking product of the psyche, has met with such profound contempt. ~Carl Jung, CW 7, Para 21

It should never be forgotten—and of this the Freudian school must be reminded—that morality was not brought down on tables of stone from Sinai and imposed on the people, but is a function of the human soul, as old as humanity itself. ~Carl Jung, CW 7, Para 30

Jung and Freud Meet

We met in 1906. The first day I met him it was at one o'clock in the afternoon, and we talked steadily for thirteen hours. He was the first man of real importance I had seen; no one else could compare with him. I found him extremely shrewd, intelligent, and altogether remarkable.

But my first impressions of him were somewhat confused; I could not quite make him out. I found him, though, absolutely serious about his sex theory, and in his attitude there was nothing trivial to be found. It made a great impression on me, but still I had grave doubts. I told him this, and whenever I did, he always said it was because I had not had enough experience.

It was a fact that in those days I had not had enough experience upon which to form a critique. I could see that this sexual theory was enormously important to Freud, both personally and philosophically, but I could not make out whether it came from a personal bias or not, so I went away with a doubt in my mind about the whole situation.

Another impression I got in connection with this seriousness of Freud with respect to his theory of sexuality was this: He invariably sneered at spirituality as being nothing but repressed sexuality, and so I said if one were committed fully to the logic of that position, then one must say that our whole civilization is farcical, nothing but a morbid creation due to repressed sexuality. He said, "Yes, so it is, and its being so is just a curse of fate we cannot help." My mind was quite unwilling to settle there, but still I could not argue it out with him. ~Carl Jung, 1925 Seminar, p. 15-26

Jung was 31 when he met Freud and was very impressed by the forcefulness of his personality. Later Jung realized that this was related to Freud's inflexibility and total inability to change and reverse course when new information would require it. Freud committed to the idea that sexuality is the basis of all psychological forces in the human mind. Jung wrote: "*He invariably sneered at spirituality as being nothing but repressed sexuality, and so I said if one were committed fully to the logic of that position, then one must say that our whole civilization is farcical, nothing but a morbid creation due to repressed sexuality. He said, "Yes, so it is, and its being so is just a curse of fate we cannot help." My mind was quite unwilling to settle there, but still I could not argue it out with him.*"

Despite the admiration the early Jung had felt for Freud he was unwilling to follow Freud in his desolate intellectuality where spirituality is nothing but a morbid interest, and civilization's investment in religion is nothing but a farce. Freud talked about sexuality with religious fervor, like it was his God. To Freud sexuality was omnipresent, powerful, and the source of everything in the human mind. All life came from sexuality.

As soon as he got to know Freud a little better Jung came to fully realize the dead end impasse that divided their thinking and perspective on the most basic idea of what is a human being. Jung wrote about his conversations with Freud when Freud was talking about sexuality: "*A peculiar emotional quality would come into his face*" … "*as a man would talk who had undergone a conversion*".

It seems to me that Jung could never develop a friendship with Freud whom he described as follows: "*One might say Freud consists of bitterness, every word being loaded with it. His attitude was the bitterness of the person who is entirely misunderstood, and his manner always seemed to say, "If they don't understand they must be stamped into Hell."* Jung had such a marvelous talent for describing people perceptively from within.

I find it ironic that Freud's spontaneous and intense emotion reveals that he is not actually an atheist and not actually a scientific materialist! To feel that you want to stamp some people into Hell do you not then demonstrate that you believe that there is one? Jung would agree with me when he wrote: "*Freud, for all his repudiation of spirituality, has in reality a mystical attitude toward sexuality.*" For "mystical" we can read "other-worldly" or "spiritual".

To me this means that deep down Freud was a believer in the existence of the other world. He was secretly a dualist in disguise. I react to this because it reminds me what another well-known psychologist of the twentieth century, Charles E. Osgood, said to me: "*Leon, you are a dualist in disguise!*" This was in 1964 when Osgood and I were administering a research grant in cross-cultural psycholinguistics at the University of Illinois. Osgood's remark was provoked by something I said about the nature of meaning. I'm quoting from an interview I had in August 2007 with the *New Yorker* magazine and am including two extra paragraphs to put dualism in context with my studies of Jung and Swedenborg:

> *Dr. Osgood was a past President of the prestigious American Psychological Association and was known for developing ways of measuring empirically the connotative meaning of words and objects. He was a staunch empiricist and materialist, holding up monism for science, which is the unproven belief that thoughts and feelings were material substances in the brain. The mind was nothing but the brain. Meaning and consciousness were nothing but brain operations. But I would argue that conscious awareness of meaning and intentions existed separately from the brain and its chemical activity. Osgood then accused me of being "a dualist in disguise." This was in the 1960s.*

> *In the 1970s I worked on developing ways of mapping the semantics of talk. This was applied psycholinguistic research. I made an amazing discovery in how ideas are ordered when we think and speak. I mapped out semantic units in terms of trigrams, hexagrams, and enneads, that is, in units of three, six, and nine. I was getting closer in what I later I called*

spiritual geography, that is, the universal anatomy of the mental world in the human race.

In the 1980s I was able to give an objective scientific definition and description of dualism, thanks to my study of the Swedenborg Reports. Today I would describe dualism as the perspective on reality as two worlds, one physical or material in time, and the other mental or spiritual not in time but in eternity. Human beings are born dual citizens with a material body in time on earth connected to a mental body in eternity which is also called the afterlife. At death the physical body is detached and we continue life in eternity through our mental body. We are thus immortal. Our mental body contains the organs of the mind called affective (feelings), cognitive (thoughts), and sensorimotor (sensations). In our daily life here on earth all our thoughts and feelings are located in the mental body, not the physical brain. Thoughts and feelings are not physical objects but mental objects, and these are made of eternal spiritual substances. (You can read a copy of the full interview posted on the Web.)

Jung's perceptive insight into Freud's orientation towards his concept of sexuality, is summarized in this statement: *"Now I think sexuality is a double concept to him* [Freud]*, on the one side the mystical element, on the other mere sexuality, but the latter is the only thing that comes out in his terminology because he will not admit he has the other side."*

Everything that becomes too old becomes evil, the same is true of your highest. Learn from the suffering of the crucified God that one can also betray and crucify a God, namely the God of the old year. If a God ceases being the way of life, he must fall secretly. ~Carl Jung, Liber Novus, p. 241

Freud's public passion for atheism, materialism, and scientism is the surface veneer beneath which hides Freud's mysticism and dualism, possibly even, theism. Jung points out that Freud uses *"only concretistic sex terminology"*, and this habit "conveys the wrong idea". Jung

40

attributes Freud's "bitterness" to his perception that he is being misunderstood about sexuality despite his attempts to clarify over and over.

But Jung sees that Freud's failure at communicating his idea is due to Freud's unresolved intellectual conflict about dualism, spirituality, religion, and God. Using "concretistic" or materialistic and monist concepts in his presentation of sexuality results in Freud *"constantly working against himself"*. According to Jung, that's where Freud's failure comes from, and that's where Freud's bitterness comes from when feeling misunderstood for decades.

> *He [Man] will [mis] understand it and he will be tempted to ruin the universal life of the earth by radioactivity. Materialism and atheism, the negation of God, are indirect means to attain this goal. ~Carl Jung, Letters Vol. II, p. 163-174*

> *Death gives me durability and solidity. ~Carl Jung, Liber Novus, p. 323*

Freud's Blindness to the Unconscious

> *The fact that deity and devil belong together also plays a great role in alchemy. ~Carl Jung, Children's Dreams Seminar, p. 373*

When the psyche is not under that obligation to live in time and space alone, and obviously, it doesn't, then in to that extent the psyche is not submitted to those laws, and that means a practical continuation of life, of a sort of psychical existence, beyond time and space. ~Carl Jung, BBC broadcast, 1959, interview with John Freeman

Intellectually, Freud was standing at the pivot line and looking from time to time across the gap of materialism into the deep space of the unconscious, which is the psychic world that Jung discovered when looking within himself. Freud did not wish to look into his deep self. His ego would prevent him. Perhaps it was too scary, as we know from Jung's own experience and descriptions. Those of us with the motivation to look what's inside our personality also know from experience what the psychic world is and the collective unconscious that resides in it.

Freud did not wish to look and therefore he did not see. Jung put it clearly: "*Freud is blind to the dualism of the unconscious. He does not know that the thing that wells up has an inside and an outside, and that if you talk only of the latter you speak of the shell alone.*" Jung and Swedenborg overcame where Freud drew back. One must be willing to put pride aside and to admit to oneself that our ego is but a "shell" and our real self exists in a world that is beneath, inside, or above that shell. All of Freudian psychology is about that shell.

To reveal and understand the psychology of the real human person that lies beneath the shell we must give ourselves permission to discover the depth within. Freud's cure and success could have been Jung's psychology, but Freud chose to reject it. Jung concluded therefore: "*But there is nothing to be done about this conflict in him [Freud]; the only chance would be if he could have an experience that would make him see spirituality working inside the shell. However, his intellect would then inevitably strip it to "mere" sexuality."* As Jung asserted frequently, don't ignore the unconscious or it will bite you. Freud was attacked by his unconscious and this reduced him to inability to motivate himself to look within. Jung's compassion as well as frustration with Freud's recalcitrance can be seen in this remark by Jung: *"Freud does not know that the unconscious produces a factor to counteract the monistic principle to which he has given himself over. I find him a tragic figure, for he is a great man, but it is a fact that he runs away from himself".*

> *Sexuality dished out as sexuality is brutish; but sexuality as an expression of love is hallowed.* ~Carl Jung, CW 10, Para 234

Freud runs away from himself! Who would have believed this about the master psychologist who is an expert on unconscious motivation and psychopathology?

Towards the end of the selection presented below you will find Jung's report of his discussion with Freud about some dreams that Jung had during the days of their interaction. Freud rigidly stuck to the same note over and over again, drawing out the details from Jung's dreams in such a way that everything ended up as sexuality. Their discussion went nowhere. This final episode between the two famous psychiatrists led to "the break" that history is talking about.

Jung concluded: *"At that time, I mean when I was working on the Psychology of the Unconscious, all my dreams pointed to a break with Freud. I thought, of course, that he would accept the cellars below his cellar, but the dreams were preparing me for the contrary. Freud could see nothing in the book but resistance to the father, and the point in it to which he took the greatest exception was my contention that the libido is split and produces the thing that checks itself. This to him as a monist was utter blasphemy."*

And at that point Jung found himself alone and isolated: *"After this break I had with Freud, the pupils that I had all over the world left me and turned to Freud. They were told that my book was rubbish, and that I was a mystic, and with that the matter was settled. Suddenly I found myself completely isolated.*" As a result Jung had no choice: " I was driven to investigate fully the things within myself." This was the synchronicity of Jung's future calling him. And Jung went. How fortunate for so many of us today that he did!

The Jung Selection

It must not be thought that the task of getting a proper understanding of Freud, or, I should rather say, the task of getting him properly placed in my life, was an easy one for me.

At that time I was planning an academic career and was about to complete a work that would advance me in the university. Freud, definitely persona non grata in the medical world at that time, was hardly mentioned above a whisper by people of importance; at the congresses he was discussed only in the couloirs, never on the floor, and any connection with him was a menace to one's own reputation.

Therefore the discovery by me that my experiments in association were directly connected with Freud's theories was most unwelcome. One time while I was in my laboratory, it flashed into my mind that Freud had actually elaborated a theory which would explain my experiments.

At the same time a devil whispered in my ear that I could perfectly well publish my work without mentioning Freud, that I had worked out my experiments long before I knew of Freud, and so could claim complete independence of him as far as they went. However, I saw at once that there was an element of lying involved which I did not propose to go in for. So I openly took up the cudgels for Freud and fought for him in the subsequent congresses.

There came a certain lecturer to one of these, and gave an explanation of the neuroses entirely ignoring Freud. I protested at this, and engaged in my first fight for Freud's ideas. Later on, at another congress, there was a lecture on the compulsion neuroses, and again mention of Freud's work was omitted. This time I wrote an article in a well-known German newspaper, attacking the man.

Immediately a flood of resistances was released against me, and that man wrote me a letter and warned me that my academic future was at stake if I persisted in joining forces with Freud. Of course I felt that if I had to get an academic future at such a price, it could be damned, and I went on writing about Freud.

Freud's Untrustworthiness

All this while I continued my experiments, but still could not get myself into agreement with Freud as to the origin of all neuroses being sex-repression. Freud had published thirteen cases of hysteria, all of which were reported as the result of sexual violation. Later, when I met Freud, he said that about some of these cases, at least, he had been fooled.

One of them, for instance, was of a girl who said that when she was four years old she had been violated by her father. This man happened to be a friend of Freud's, and the latter convinced himself that the girl's story was a lie. Subsequent investigation brought out the fact that others in the series were also falsifications, but he would not retract, it having been his policy always to let things stand as he originally presented them.

There is then a certain untrustworthiness about all these earlier cases. Thus again, the famous first case that he had with Breuer, which has been so much spoken about as an example of a brilliant therapeutic success, was in reality nothing of the kind. Freud told me that he was called in to see the woman the same night that Breuer had seen her for the last time, and that she was in a bad hysterical attack, due to the breaking off of the transference.

This, then, was no cure at all in the sense in which it was originally presented, and yet it was a very interesting case, so interesting that there was no need to claim for it something that did not happen. But all of these things I did not know at that time. Besides my experiments, I was working with many cases of insanity, particularly with dementia praecox.

At that time there was no psychological viewpoint to be found in the field of psychiatry. A label was put on each case; it was said to be a degeneration here, or an atrophy there, and then it was finished—there was nothing more to be done about it. It was only among the nurses that any psychological interest in the patients could be found, and among them there were some very shrewd guesses offered as to the conditions presented; but the doctors knew none of this.

For example, there was an old case in the women's ward, a woman who was seventy-five years old, and who had lain in bed for forty years. She had been in the asylum nearly fifty years perhaps—so long, in fact, that no one remembered her entrance because the people there at the time were all dead. There was just one head nurse, who had been in the asylum thirty-five years, who knew something of this woman's early history.

This old patient could not talk, and could only eat liquid food which she took with her fingers with a peculiar shoveling movement, so that it sometimes took her two hours to get down a cup of food. When she was not feeding herself, she was making most peculiar movements with her hands and arms. I thought to myself as I looked at her, "What a terrible thing is this." But that is as far as I got with it. She was regularly presented in clinic as an old case of dementia praecox, catatonic form.

It seemed to me perfect nonsense to dispose of these extraordinary movements in that way. This case and its effect on me were typical of my whole reaction to psychiatry. For six months I was struggling desperately to find myself in it, and was all the time more and more baffled. I was deeply humiliated to see that my chief and my colleagues seemed to feel sure of themselves, and that it was only I who was drifting helplessly. My failure to understand gave me such feelings of inferiority that I could not bear to go out of the hospital. Here was I, a man with a profession which I could not rightly grasp. I therefore stayed in all the time and gave myself up to the study of my cases.

I should mention that Jung's estimate of Freud was not negative only. Jung gave Freud credit for initiating a focus on the unconscious, on bringing into psychology a new focus on the significance of dreams, and on various useful suggestions in treating certain mental and personality disorders, as indicated in the next four Jung quotes below.

> When Freud coined the phrase that the ego was "the true seat of anxiety," he was giving voice to a very true and profound intuition. ~Carl Jung, Psychological, CW 11, p. 849

> I find him a tragic figure, for he is a great man, but it is a fact that he runs away from himself. ~Carl Jung, 1925 Seminar, Lecture 3, p. 15-26

Jung Discovers the Psychogenesis of Dementia

> Late one evening, as I went through the ward and saw the old woman I have described, I asked myself, "Why should that be?" I went to the head nurse and asked if it had always been that way with that patient. "Yes," she said, "but formerly I heard from the head of the men's ward that she used to make shoes!"

> I looked up the archives and mention was made of the fact that she made movements as if making shoes. Early shoemakers held the shoe between their knees and pulled the thread through with movements exactly like the ones the old woman used to make. One can still see them doing it in certain primitive places. Some time after this the patient died. Then her brother three years older than herself turned up.

> "Why did your sister go insane?" I asked him. He told me she had been in love with a shoemaker, but for some reason the man did not want to marry her, and that she had gone insane. She had kept alive the vision of him with those movements. This was my first inkling of the psychogenesis of dementia praecox. Then I kept careful watch over the cases and noted the psychogenetic factors.

It became clear to me that Freud's conceptions could throw light on these problems. This is the origin of The Psychology of Dementia Praecox. I did not meet with much sympathy for my ideas. In fact, my colleagues laughed at me. It was another example of the difficulty felt by certain people when asked to consider a new idea.

Jung Discovers the Relevance of the Unconscious

In 1906 I worked out very carefully a case of dementia praecox of suppression, or of inferiority as we would say now. I took down her material in great detail, and often while we were talking her voices would interrupt, saying something like this: "Tell the doctor that all you are saying is bunk, and that he need pay no attention to it." Or sometimes when she would be protesting violently at being kept in the asylum, the voices would say, "You know perfectly well you are insane and belong right where you are."

Naturally she had great resistances to the voices. I got the idea that the unconscious was entirely on top, and that her ego-consciousness had gone into the unconscious. I discovered further, to my astonishment and bewilderment that the ideas of megalomania and those of depreciation came of one and the same source. The ideas of depreciation were those of being ill-treated or wronged or of being bad. These I called self-depreciation, while the ideas of megalomania I called self-appreciation.

At the beginning I held it for impossible that the unconscious could produce the opposites together in this way for I was still on the Schopenhauer-Hartmann-Freud trail. The unconscious was only an urge and could not display a conflict within itself. Then I thought perhaps the two came from different levels of the unconscious, but that would not work; and finally I had to admit that the woman's mind was using both principles at once. Later cases corroborated my findings.

For example, I had the case of a very intelligent lawyer who was suffering from paranoia. In these cases there is just one idea about which they are insane, namely persecution; otherwise they are adapted to reality. The case develops somewhat as follows: A man thinks he notices people talking about him; then he asks himself why, and answers it by saying that he must be someone important whom other people want to crush.

Little by little he finds he is a Messiah who must be annihilated. The man of whom I am speaking was dangerous in that he had attempted one murder, and when he was free attempted another. He had held an important political position, and one could talk to him. He hated the doctors and spent his time cursing them. Once he broke down with me and said, "I know that alienists are the very finest people."

Then he fainted. This moment came after I had worked with him three hours. When he came to again, he was in his old state of depreciation. The depreciation is produced as compensation to the megalomania. I insist on this point so much because it is back of the Yea and Nay in the unconscious; in other words, the unconscious contains the pairs of opposites. Through this book on dementia praecox I came to Freud.

Jung: Sexuality Is Freud's God

A third impression of those days involves things that became clear to me only much later, things that I thought out fully only after our friendship was gone. When Freud talked of sexuality it was as though he were talking of God—as a man would talk who had undergone a conversion. It was like the Indians talking of the sun with tears in their eyes.

I remember one Indian coming up softly behind me while I was looking at the mountain over the pueblo, and saying quite suddenly in my ear, "Don't you think all life is coming from the mountain?" It was just in that way that Freud talked of sexuality. A peculiar emotional quality would come into his face, and the cause of it I was at a loss to understand.

Finally I seemed to make it out through the consideration of something else that remained obscure to me then, namely Freud's bitterness. One might say Freud consists of bitterness, every word being loaded with it. His attitude was the bitterness of the person who is entirely misunderstood, and his manner always seemed to say, "If they don't understand they must be stamped into Hell."

I noticed this in him the first time I met him, and always saw it in him, but I could not find the connection with his attitude toward sexuality. The explanation seems to me to be this: Freud, for all his repudiation of spirituality, has in reality a mystical attitude toward sexuality.

When one protested to him that a certain poem could not be understood on a sexual basis exclusively, he would say, "No, certainly not, that is psychosexuality." But when analyzing the poem, he would pull out this thread and that, and so on until nothing was left but sexuality. Now I think sexuality is a double concept to him, on the one side the mystical element, on the other mere sexuality, but the latter is the only thing that comes out in his terminology because he will not admit he has the other side.

That he has the other side, I think, is obvious from the way he showed his emotions. And so he is forever defeating his own purpose. He wants to teach that sexuality contains spirituality looked at from within, but he uses only concretistic sex terminology and conveys just the wrong idea. His bitterness comes from this fact of constantly working against himself, for there is no bitterness worse than that of a man who is his own worst enemy.

Freud is blind to the dualism of the unconscious. He does not know that the thing that wells up has an inside and an outside, and that if you talk only of the latter you speak of the shell alone.

But there is nothing to be done about this conflict in him; the only chance would be if he could have an experience that would make him see spirituality working inside the shell. However, his intellect would then inevitably strip it to "mere" sexuality. I tried to present to him cases showing other factors than sexual ones but always he would have it that there was nothing there save repressed sexuality. As I said, such terribly bitter people are always those who work against themselves.

When I work against myself I project the uncertainty and terror that I feel. If I am to avoid this, the one thing to settle is myself. Freud does not know that the unconscious produces a factor to counteract the monistic principle to which he has given himself over.

I find him a tragic figure, for he is a great man, but it is a fact that he runs away from himself. He never asks himself why he has to talk about sex all the time, and in this running away from himself he is like any other artist. In fact, creative people are usually like that. These thoughts came to me, as I said, chiefly after I had broken with Freud. I give them to you because as you know, my relation to Freud has long since become a matter of public discussion, and so I must present my view of it.

I came away from my first visit to Freud feeling that the sexual factor must be taken most seriously. Somewhat bewildered, I began to look at my cases again and kept pretty quiet. In 1909 Freud and I were both invited to Clark University, and we were together daily for about seven weeks. We analyzed dreams each day, and it was then that I got an impression, a fatal one, of his limitations.

I had two dreams out of which he could not make head or tail. Of course I did not mind that, for the very greatest person is going to have that experience with dreams some time or other. It was just a human limitation, and I would never have taken it as a reason for not going on; on the contrary, I wanted very much to go on—I felt myself to be his son. Then something happened which put a stop to it. Freud had a dream on an important theme which I cannot mention.

I analyzed it and said there was more to be said if he would give me some points about his private life. He looked at me with a peculiar expression of suspicion in his eyes and said, "I could tell you more but I can't risk my authority. "Then I knew further analysis was impossible because he put authority above truth. I said I would have to stop there, and I never asked him again for material.

You must understand that I speak here quite objectively, but I must include this experience with Freud, because it is the most important factor in my relation to him. He could not bear any criticism whatsoever.

As Freud could only partially handle my dreams, the amount of symbolical material in them increased as it always does until it is understood. If one remains with a narrow point of view about the dream material, there comes a feeling of dissociation and one feels blind and deaf. When this happens to an isolated man he petrifies.

On my way back from America, I had a dream that was the origin of my book on the Psychology of the Unconscious. In those times I had no idea of the collective unconscious; I thought of the conscious as of a room above, with the unconscious as a cellar underneath and then the earth wellspring, that is, the body, sending up the instincts. These instincts tend to disagree with our conscious ideals and so we keep them down. That is the figure I had always used for myself, and then came this dream which I hope I can tell without being too personal.

Jung's Dream Foreshadows Break With Freud

I dreamed I was in a medieval house, a big, complicated house with many rooms, passages, and stairways.

I came in from the street and went down into a vaulted Gothic room, and from there into a cellar. I thought to myself that now I was at the bottom, but then I found a square hole. With a lantern in my hand I peeped down this hole, and saw stairs leading further down, and down these I climbed.

They were dusty stairs, very much worn, and the air was sticky, the whole atmosphere very uncanny. I came to another cellar, this one of very ancient structure, perhaps Roman, and again there was a hole through which I could look down into a tomb filled with prehistoric pottery, bones, and skulls; as the dust was undisturbed, I thought I had made a great discovery. There I woke up.

Freud said this dream meant that there were certain people associated with me whom I wanted dead, and buried under two cellars, but I thought the meaning was entirely elsewhere though I could not make it out. I kept thinking this way: The cellar is the unconscious, but what is the medieval house?

This I did not make out until much later. But there was something below both cellars even—that is, remains of prehistoric man. What does that mean?

I had a strongly impersonal feeling about the dream. Involuntarily I began to make fantasies about it, though I did not then know anything about the principle of fantasizing in order to bring up unconscious material. I said to myself, "Isn't it fine to make excavations. Where am I going to have a chance to do that?" And actually when I came home I looked up a place where excavations were being made, and went to it. But of course that did not satisfy me.

My thoughts then beginning to turn to the East, I began to read about excavations being made in Babylonia. My interest went to books, and I came upon a German book called Mythology and Symbolism. I went through the three or four volumes at top speed, reading like mad, in fact, until I became as bewildered as ever I had been in the clinic. I had left the hospital, by the way, in 1909, after being there eight years, but now it seemed to me I was living in an insane asylum of my own making.

I went about with all these fantastic figures: centaurs, nymphs, satyrs, gods and goddesses, as though they were patients and I was analyzing them. I read a Greek or a Negro myth as if a lunatic were telling me his anamnesis—I lost myself in puzzling what it could possibly mean. Slowly out of all this came the Psychology of the Unconscious, for in the midst of it I came upon the Miller fantasies, and they acted like a catalyzer upon all the material I had gathered together in my mind.

I saw in Miss Miller a person who, like myself, had had mythological fantasies, fantasies and dreams of a thoroughly impersonal character. Their impersonality I readily recognized, as well as the fact that they must come from the lower "cellars," though I did not give the name of collective unconscious to them. This then is the way the book grew up.

While working on the book I was haunted by bad dreams. I feel that I must speak of my dreams even though one is unavoidably personal to a degree when one does so. But dreams have influenced all the important changes in my life and theories.

Thus for example I came to study medicine by reason of a dream, it having been my firm intention at first to become an archeologist. With this in view I had entered my name in the list of students of philosophy at the University, but then came this dream, and I changed everything.

At that time, I mean when I was working on the Psychology of the Unconscious, all my dreams pointed to a break with Freud. I thought, of course, that he would accept the cellars below his cellar, but the dreams were preparing me for the contrary.

Freud could see nothing in the book but resistance to the father, and the point in it to which he took the greatest exception was my contention that the libido is split and produces the thing that checks itself. This to him as a monist was utter blasphemy.

From this attitude of Freud's I felt more than ever convinced that his idea of God was placed in sexuality, and that libido is to him only an urge in one direction.

As a matter of fact, however, I think it can be shown that there is a will to die as well as a will to live. We prepare ourselves for death when we reach the summit of life; or, to put it in another way, after the age of thirty-five, let us say, we begin to know that cooler winds are blowing—at first we don't understand, but later we cannot escape the meaning.

After this break I had with Freud, the pupils that I had all over the world left me and turned to Freud. They were told that my book was rubbish, and that I was a mystic, and with that the matter was settled.

Suddenly I found myself completely isolated.

This, however disadvantageous it may have been, had also an advantage for me as an introvert; that is it encouraged the vertical movement of the libido. Cut off from the horizontal movement which activity in the outside world brings, I was driven to investigate fully the things within myself.

When I finished the Psychology of the Unconscious, I had a peculiarly lucid moment in which I surveyed my path as far as I had come. I thought: "Now you have the key to mythology and you have the power to unlock all doors." But then something within me said: "Why unlock all these doors?"

And then I found myself asking what I had done after all. I had written a book about the hero, I had explained the myths of past peoples, but what about my own myth? I had to admit I had none; I knew theirs but none of my own, nor did anyone else have one today. Moreover, we were without an understanding of the unconscious.

Around these reflections, as around a central core, grew all the ideas that came to partial expression in the book on types.

~Carl Jung, 1925 Seminar, Lecture 3, p. 15-26

Note: The text of the Jung selection above was <u>posted on the Web</u> and I found it in 2016.

One is always in the dark about one's own personality. One needs others to get to know oneself.

Carl and Emma Jung were married in 1903

The world of the Gods is made manifest in spirituality and in sexuality. The celestial ones appear in spirituality, the earthly in sexuality. ~Carl Jung, Liber Novus, p. 352

Love is a force of destiny whose power reaches from heaven to hell. ~Carl Jung, CW 10, Para 198

One is always in the dark about one's own personality. One needs others to get to know oneself. Having said this—I actually started out by simply doing routine scientific work.

I always followed the motto that it is worth doing something only if you do it right! The incentives for my creative work are rooted in my temperament. Diligence and a strong desire for knowledge accompanied me throughout life. I do not derive any satisfaction from knowing things superficially: I want to know them thoroughly.

When I came to the conclusion that I had only hazy notions of the primitives, and that it was not possible to acquire full knowledge about them through books, I started traveling in Africa, New Mexico, and India. For the same reason I also started learning Swahili. ~Carl Jung, C.G. Jung Speaking: Interviews and Encounters, p. 164-167

There's a famous story that Robert Bly tells about Carl Jung who, whenever a friend reported enthusiastically, 'I have just been promoted!' Jung would say, 'I'm very sorry to hear that; but if we all stick together, I think we will get through it.' On the other hand, if a friend arrived depressed and ashamed, saying, 'I've just been fired,' Jung would say, 'Let's open a bottle of wine; this is wonderful news; something good will happen now.' http://toko-pa.com/2014/05/12/loss-of-identity-a-summoning-of-the-numinous/

My soul leads me into the desert, into the desert of my own self. ~Carl Jung, Liber Novus, p. 235

 ## From the New York Times About Jung

Carl Jung founded the field of analytical psychology and, along with Sigmund Freud, was responsible for popularizing the idea that a person's interior life merited not just attention but dedicated exploration — a notion that has since propelled tens of millions of people into self-analysis. Freud, who started as Jung's mentor and later became his rival, generally viewed the unconscious mind as a warehouse for repressed desires, which could then be codified and pathologized and treated. Jung, over time, came to see the psyche as an inherently more spiritual and fluid place, an ocean that could be fished for enlightenment and healing.

Whether or not he would have wanted it this way, Jung — who regarded himself as a scientist — is today remembered more as a countercultural icon, a proponent of spirituality outside religion and the ultimate champion of dreamers and seekers everywhere, which has earned him both posthumous respect and posthumous ridicule. Jung's ideas laid the foundation for the widely used Myers-Briggs personality test and influenced the creation of Alcoholics Anonymous. His central tenets — the existence of a collective unconscious and the power of archetypes — have seeped into the larger domain of New Age thinking while remaining more at the fringes of mainstream psychology.

A big man with wire-rimmed glasses, a booming laugh and a penchant for the experimental, Jung was interested in the psychological aspects of séances, of astrology, of witchcraft. He could be jocular and also impatient. He was a dynamic speaker, an empathic listener. He had a famously magnetic appeal with women. Working at Zurich's Burghölzli psychiatric hospital, Jung listened intently to the ravings of schizophrenics, believing they held clues to both personal and universal truths. At home, in his spare time, he pored over Dante, Goethe, Swedenborg and Nietzsche. He began to study mythology and world cultures, applying what he learned to the live feed from the unconscious — claiming that dreams offered a rich and symbolic narrative coming from the depths of the psyche. Somewhere along the way, he started to view the human soul — not just the mind and the body — as requiring specific care and development, an idea that pushed him into a province long occupied by poets and priests but not so much by medical doctors and empirical scientists.

Jung soon found himself in opposition not just to Freud but also to most of his field, the psychiatrists who constituted the dominant culture at the time, speaking the clinical language of symptom and diagnosis behind the deadbolts of asylum wards. Separation was not easy. As his convictions began to crystallize, Jung, who was at that point an outwardly successful and ambitious man with a young family, a thriving private practice and a big, elegant house on the shores of Lake Zurich, felt his own psyche starting to teeter and slide, until finally he was dumped into what would become a life-altering crisis.

What happened next to Carl Jung has become, among Jungians and other scholars, the topic of enduring legend and controversy. It has been characterized variously as a creative illness, a descent into the underworld, a bout with insanity, a narcissistic self-deification, a transcendence, a midlife breakdown and an inner disturbance mirroring the upheaval of World War I. Whatever the case, in 1913, Jung, who was then 38, got lost in the soup of his own psyche. He was haunted by troubling visions and heard inner voices. Grappling with the horror of some of what he saw, he worried in moments that he was, in his own words, "menaced by a psychosis" or "doing a schizophrenia."

He later would compare this period of his life — this "confrontation with the unconscious," as he called it — to a mescaline experiment. He described his visions as coming in an "incessant stream." He likened them to rocks falling on his head, to thunderstorms, to molten lava. "I often had to cling to the table," he recalled, "so as not to fall apart."

Had he been a psychiatric patient, Jung might well have been told he had a nervous disorder and encouraged to ignore the circus going on in his head. But as a psychiatrist, and one with a decidedly maverick streak, he tried instead to tear down the wall between his rational self and his psyche. For about six years, Jung worked to prevent his conscious mind from blocking out what his unconscious mind wanted to show him. Between appointments with patients, after dinner with his wife and children, whenever there was a spare hour or two, Jung sat in a book-lined office on the second floor of his home and actually induced hallucinations — what he called "active imaginations." "In order to grasp the fantasies which were stirring in me 'underground,' " Jung wrote later in his book "Memories, Dreams, Reflections," "I knew that I had to let myself plummet down into them." He found himself in a liminal place, as full of creative abundance as it was of potential ruin, believing it to be the same borderlands traveled by both lunatics and great artists.

...

The book tells the story of Jung trying to face down his own demons as they emerged from the shadows. The results are humiliating, sometimes unsavory. In it, Jung travels the land of the dead, falls in love with a woman he later realizes is his sister, gets squeezed by a giant serpent and, in one terrifying moment, eats the liver of a little child. ("I swallow with desperate efforts — it is impossible — once again and once again — I almost faint — it is done.") At one point, even the devil criticizes Jung as hateful.

He worked on his red book — and he called it just that, the Red Book — on and off for about 16 years, long after his personal crisis had passed, but he never managed to finish it. He actively fretted over it, wondering whether to have it published and face ridicule from his scientifically oriented peers or to put it in a drawer and forget it. Regarding the significance of what the book contained, however, Jung was unequivocal. "All my works, all my creative activity," he would recall later, "has come from those initial fantasies and dreams."

...

Jungian analysis revolves largely around writing down your dreams (or drawing them) and bringing them to the analyst — someone who is patently good with both symbols and people — to be scoured for personal and archetypal meaning. Borrowing from Jung's own experiences, analysts often encourage clients to experiment on their own with active imagination, to summon a waking dreamscape and to interact with whatever, or whoever, surfaces there.

Analysis is considered to be a form of self-analysis, and many analysts are in fact trained also as psychotherapists, but in its purist form, a Jungian analyst eschews clinical talk of diagnoses and recovery in favor of broader (and some might say fuzzier) goals of self-discovery and wholeness — a maturation process Jung himself referred to as "individuation." Perhaps as a result, Jungian analysis has a distinct appeal to people in midlife. "The purpose of analysis is not treatment," Martin explained to me. "That's the purpose of self-analysis. The purpose of analysis," he added, a touch grandly, "is to give life back to someone who's lost it." ~Sara Corbett, The Holy Grail of the Unconscious, The New York Times Magazine, Sept. 16, 2009

It was actually through my therapeutic work that I began to understand the essence of the Christian faith. ~Carl Jung, Letters Vol. II, p. 631

I think unconsciously. ~Carl Jung, C.G. Jung Speaking: Interviews and Encounters, p. 167

I assure you it was precisely through my analytic work that I arrived at an understanding not only of the Christian religion but, I may say, of all religions. ~Carl Jung, Letters Vol. II, p. 631

If I could not stand criticism I would have been dead long ago, since I have had nothing but criticism for 60 years. ~Carl Jung, Letters Vol. II, p. 583

It is surely not the divine will in man that he should be something which he is not, for when one looks into nature, one sees that it is most definitely the divine will that everything should be what it is. ~Carl Jung, Visions Seminar, p. 569

I am glad I am Jung, not Jungian. I can only hope and wish that no one becomes "Jungian." I stand for no doctrine, but describe facts and put forward certain views which I hold worthy of discussion. ~Carl Jung, Letters Vol. 1, p. 404-406

Jung Resources on the Web

I want to acknowledge the valuable scholarly contribution of Lewis Lafontaine who posts on a daily basis numerous Jung quotes on his Facebook Group page and on his Web blogs about Jung. I re-present many of these quotes in this book.

Carl Jung Depth Psychology Facebook Group:
https://www.facebook.com/groups/56536297291/

Carl Jung Depth Psychology Blog:
http://www.blogger.com/home

See also:

Jung Depth Psychology Web Blog:
http://carljungdepthpsychology.blogspot.com/

Lewis Lafontaine Google+:
https://plus.google.com/102529939687199578205/posts

LinkedIn: http://bit.ly/1XeGwEj

Jung on Facebook:
https://www.facebook.com/Carl-Jung-326016020781946/
https://www.facebook.com/groups/792124710867966/

Purrington's Pinterest Boards on Jung:
https://www.pinterest.com/purrington104/

Carl Jung on WordPress Blog:
https://carljungdepthpsychology.wordpress.com/

Jung's dreams culled from his collected works: http://www.carl-g-jung.de/english/dreams.html

END OF CHAPTER 1

Chapter 2
About Emanuel Swedenborg
(1688-1772)

I admire Swedenborg as a great scientist and a great mystic at the same time. His life and work has always been of great interest to me and I read about seven fat volumes of his writings when I was a medical student. ~Carl Jung

We are because God is.
~Swedenborg, DP 46

Emanuel Swedenborg was a Swedish scientist, inventor, and theologian who made significant discoveries in many of the natural sciences, including astronomy, anatomy, geology, and mineralogy. At age fifty-five, his intensive search for answers to ultimate questions culminated in an awakening that gave him a unique insight into the workings of the spiritual world. He spent the remainder of his life writing about his experiences and how human beings can come to a deeper awareness of the divine.

Swedenborg's ideas have influenced people as diverse as Helen Keller, Johnny Appleseed, William Blake, Henry James, Ralph Waldo Emerson, D.T. Suzuki, Jorge Luis Borges, and Dr. Mehmet Oz. The continuing appeal of his thought undoubtedly lies in his insights into the afterlife, concepts of divine love, and focus on personal and social development.

In his earlier career Swedenborg immersed himself in the sciences and other secular pursuits, though did not abandon his early religious training. He retained his acceptance of God as the all pervasive, causal force in the universe. All evidence indicates that he consistently followed the advice which his father gave to him upon leaving Uppsala to accept an appointment in another diocese: "I beg you most earnestly that you fear and love God above all else," the Bishop said, "for without this fear of God all other training, all study, all learning is of no account, indeed quite harmful."

For thirty-one years Swedenborg served as a valued member of the Swedish Board of Mines. The Board met regularly and made decisions affecting all aspects of the mine industry. Swedenborg sometimes received leaves of absence for travel and study but attended Board meetings faithfully when he was in Sweden. As Assessor of mines Swedenborg's responsibilities included inspecting mines and rendering detailed reports on the quality and amount of mined ore.

In 1745 in London, while dining alone at an inn where he often went, Swedenborg noted that the room seemed to grow dark. He then saw a vision, and an apparition spoke to him. When the room cleared again Swedenborg went home to his apartment, considerably stirred by his experience. During that night he again saw the vision. A spirit reappeared and spoke with him regarding the need for a human person to serve as the means by which God would further reveal himself to men in somewhat the manner of the biblical visions of the Old Testament.

Swedenborg came to believe that God had called him to bring a new revelation to the world, and from 1745 until his death twenty-seven years later he spent the bulk of his time adding theological works to his already lengthy scientific and philosophical writings. Few transcendent experiences recorded in human history encompass such a sweeping claim.

In 1768, Swedenborg, eighty years of age but in excellent health and spirits, set out on the next-to-last extensive journey of his life on earth. Many previous trips had taken him all over Europe including Italy, France, Germany, Holland, and England. During the summer he spent many hours working on his last great theological work, a study entitled True Christian Religion. He also enjoyed walking in the nearby parks, talking with acquaintances, and visiting friends.

Several friends visited Swedenborg during March and urged him to make a final statement regarding the truth or falsity of the new revelation which had been flowing from his pen for so many years. Swedenborg answered pointedly:

> *"I have written nothing but the truth, as you will have more and more confirmed to you all the days of your life, provided you keep close to the Lord and faithfully serve Him alone by shunning evils of all kinds as sins against Him and diligently searching His Word which from beginning to end bears incontestable witness to the truth of the doctrines I have delivered to the world."*

On another occasion, in answer to a similar question, Swedenborg said:

> *"As truly as you see me before your eyes, so true is everything that I have written; and I could have said more had it been permitted. When you enter eternity you will see everything, and then you and I shall have much to talk about."*

Some people have called Swedenborg a "mystic", a "visionary", a "seer", "prophet of the soul", or "clairvoyant medium". Many see him as a "theologian". I call Swedenborg a scientist.

Here are some more epithets about Swedenborg used by various well known critics (see list below):

- the Buddha of the North
- making the deepest mark upon the religions of future ages of any man that ever walked the earth
- advanced scientist and thinker

- a fountain of life and my strongest incitement to overcome limitations
- the sanest and most far-reaching intellect this age has ever known
- the greatest and highest human mind
- a great scientist and a great mystic at the same time
- the sanest and most far-reaching intellect this age has ever known
- the most extraordinary person on earth
- epitomizes all the religions - or rather the one religion - of humanity
- the only light that has been cast on the other life
- a man beautiful, lovable and tragical
- More truths are confessed in his writings than in those of any other man
- One of the loftiest minds in the realm of mind
- All other writers seem moving in the dark with tapers in hand, groping their way, while he moves in the broad daylight of the sun

I will show throughout this book in what way Swedenborg was a scientist. Over a period of 27 years in his dual consciousness Swedenborg collected a unique database of information or ethnography of the spiritual world. He is describing what he saw empirically, no less than an anthropologist who is writing a report on an isolated tribe in Australia where he spent two decades studying the culture, language, and social life of the tribe.

With respect to religion Swedenborg defines "faith" in two modalities: "blind faith" and "rational faith". The first is persuasive and dogmatic, while the second is empirical and psychological. Rational faith consists of only propositions that can be proven on the basis of observation and methodological consistency. For instance, in Swedenborg we find a medical or anatomical definition of "evil" and "sin" rather than a dogmatic judgment that follows from a given creed.

Swedenborg's science is "theistic" and involves God's immediate, active, and personal intervention in the sequence of events in an individual's life, which also includes the feelings, emotions, and thoughts that the individual has in daily life. Within this dual reality sin and evil is a category of feeling and thinking in such a way as to be detrimental the survival of the individual and society. An example is crime, which is defined as bad not from moral judgment but from societal functioning. There are biological reasons and justifications for promoting and maintaining forces that oppose sin and evil in society, such as honesty, altruism, justice, mutual love and respect. The motivation for being good and useful requires the motivation to avoid hurting others.

If you examine what respected and well-regarded writers and commentators have written about Swedenborg, shown below, you will understand how deeply they were affected by Swedenborg's scientific thinking about God, the afterlife, sin, and religion. He is called a "divine teacher", a bright shining spiritual sun", "a source of inspiration", "advanced scientist and thinker", and "the sanest and most far-reaching intellect this age has ever known".

The first thing of charity is to shun evils.
~Swedenborg, The True Christian Religion, TCR
535

What Some Notables in History Have Said About Swedenborg

Some critics of Swedenborg's reports of the afterlife have simply labeled him as psychotic or delusional. Others have seen in his works as a new religion. Still others, like those listed below, have seen him as remarkable genius. This high assessment is due not so much to his visions per se as to his rational presentation of the dual world and how it affects our mind and development. In Swedenborg's Writings they find a new, coherent and systematic explanation of reality, God, life after death, and the nature of the human mind.

Here is a list that indicates Swedenborg's high reputation and status as a thinker among some of the best known literary critics and writers of the 18th and 19th centuries in Western literature:

Honoré de Balzac (1799-1850)
French novelist; declared that Swedenborgianism was his religion.

Charles Baudelaire (1821-1867)
French poet; fascinated by Swedenborg's doctrine of
'correspondences'; used this as a cornerstone of his aesthetic
metaphysics.

William Blake (1757-1827)
Poet and artist; called Swedenborg a "divine teacher".

Elizabeth Barrett Browning (1806-1861) and Robert Browning (1812-1889)
Renowned English poets read Swedenborg's Conjugial Love together
in Florence early in their marriage.

Thomas Carlyle (1795-1881)
Eminent Scottish essayist; described Swedenborg as 'one of the
spiritual suns that will shine brighter as the years go on.'

Fyodor Dostoevsky (1821-1881)
Great Russian novelist; his books contain clear Swedenborgian
teaching about the spiritual world, particularly that hell is always a
voluntary spiritual state.

Ralph Waldo Emerson (1803-1882)
American poet, philosopher and essayist; His biographical essay,
'Swedenborg, or the Mystic' was published in his Representative Men.

Johann Wolfgang von Goethe (1749-1832)
Great German poet, dramatist, novelist, essayist and scientist;
students of his letters and poetry have found evidence of familiarity
with both scientific and theological works of Swedenborg)

Immanuel Kant (1724-1804)
(great German Idealist philosopher became aware of Swedenborg's
reputation as a clairvoyant and seer in the early 1760s; wrote a
frequently cited scathing attack on Swedenborg entitled Dreams of a
Spirit-Seer (1766)

Joseph Sheridan Le Fanu (1814-1873)
(Anglo-Irish novelist and short-story writer; made his living as a journalist; Swedenborg's influence on his writing may be seen most strongly in his best-known novel Uncle Silas)

Oscar V de Lubicz Milosz (1877-1939)
Lithuanian diplomat and French poet, he was one of the last great hermetic thinkers of the twentieth century and a student of Swedenborg.

George MacDonald (1824-1905)
Scottish novelist, poet and 'myth-maker'; inspired by Swedenborg and Blake.

Czeslaw Milosz (1911-2004)
Lithuanian-born poet, novelist, essayist, translator, critic and scholar; won the Nobel Prize for Literature in 1980; acknowledged Swedenborg as one of his main sources of inspiration.

Coventry Patmore (1823-1896)
English poet; was inspired by his reading of Swedenborg's Conjugial Love; acknowledges the influence of Swedenborg on his work and may be seen in his later volume The Unknown Eros.

Arthur Schopenhauer (1788-1860)
German Idealist philosopher; fascinated by Swedenborg and employs terminology in relation to the connection between the will and the understanding.

DT Suzuki (1870-1966)
Internationally known Japanese Zen Buddhist scholar; translated into Japanese several Swedenborg books; described Swedenborg as 'the Buddha of the North'.

Alfred Lord Tennyson (1809-1892)
Most popular poet of the Victorian age; lifelong reader of Swedenborg.

Walt Whitman (1819-1892)
Leading American poet of the nineteenth century; wrote that Swedenborg will probably 'make the deepest and broadest mark

upon the religions of future ages here, of any man that ever walked the earth.'

James John Garth Wilkinson (1812-1899)
(Homoeopathic physician, translator and biographer of Swedenborg and a writer on a variety of religious, medical and social topics)

Calvin Coolidge, American President (1872-1933)
"I desire to express my deep interest in the work and life of this advanced scientist and thinker Swedenborg, who was a pioneer two hundred years ago in much of the progress and advancement in mechanical, biological and medical science of the present day, and whose great learning and deep understanding of the mysteries of life was supplemented by the strong religious faith which has had devout followers many generations after the founder's death."

Helen Keller, Author (1880-1968)
I acknowledge my profound indebtedness to Emanuel Swedenborg for a richer interpretation of the Bible, a deeper understanding of Christianity, and a precious sense of the divine presence in the world. His message has meant so much to me. It has given color and reality and unity to my thought of the life to come; it has exalted my ideas of love, truth and usefulness; it has been my strongest incitement to overcome limitations. Swedenborg's Divine Love and Wisdom is a fountain of life I am always happy to be near."

Dr. Carl Gustav Jung, Psychologist (1875-1961)
"I admire Swedenborg as a great scientist and a great mystic at the same time. His life and work has always been of great interest to me and I read about seven fat volumes of his writings when I was a medical student."

Henry James Sr., Author (1811-1882)
"Emanuel Swedenborg had the sanest and most far-reaching intellect this age has ever known."

William Butler Yeats, Poet (1865-1939)
"It was indeed Swedenborg who affirmed for the modern world, as against the abstract reasoning of the learned, the doctrine and practice of the desolate places, of shepherds and midwives, and

discovered a world of spirits where there was a scenery like that of the earth, human forms, grotesque or beautiful, senses that knew pleasure and pain, marriage and war, all that could be painted upon canvas or put into stories."

Sir Arthur Conan Doyle, Author (1859-1930)
"The great Swedish seer Emanuel Swedenborg has some claim to be the father of our new knowledge of supernal matters. When the first rays of the rising sun of spiritual knowledge fell upon the earth they illuminated the greatest and highest human mind before they shed their light on lesser men. That mountain peak of mentality was this great religious reformer and clairvoyant medium..."

Samuel Taylor Coleridge, Poet (1772-1834)
"Of the too limited time which my ill-health and the exigencies of the today leave in my power, I have given the larger portion to the works of Swedenborg. I remember nothing in Lord Bacon superior, few passages equal, either in depth of thought, or in richness, dignity and felicity of diction, or in the weightiness of the truths contained in these articles. I can venture to assert that as a moralist Swedenborg is above all praise; and that as a naturalist, psychologist and theologian, he has strong and varied claims on the gratitude and admiration of the professional and philosophical world."

Jorge Luis Borges, Author (1899-1986)
"Of another famous Scandinavian, Charles XII, Voltaire was able to write that he was the most extraordinary person on earth. The superlative mode is an imprudence in that it implies less conviction than mere polemic; but I would apply Voltaire's characterization, not to Charles XII but to that most mysterious of his subjects, Emanuel Swedenborg."

Honoré de Balzac, Author (1799-1850)
"Do you know, I have come back to Swedenborg after vast studies of all religions, and after reading all the works published within the last sixty years? Swedenborg undoubtedly epitomizes all the religions - or rather the one religion - of humanity.

Elizabeth Barret Browning, Poet (1806-1861)

"To my mind the only light that has been cast on the other life is found in Swedenborg's philosophy. It explains much that was incomprehensible."

Thomas Carlyle, Clergyman (1795-1881)
"Swedenborg was a man of great and indisputable cultivation, strong mathematical intellect, and the most pious, seraphic turn of mind; a man beautiful, lovable and tragical to me. More truths are confessed in his writings than in those of any other man. One of the loftiest minds in the realm of mind. One of the spiritual suns that will shine brighter as the years go on."

Walter M. Horton, Professor of Philosophy of Christianity (Oberlin College) (1903-1967)
"In the age of 'one-eyed' reason, as it has been called, Swedenborg was among the very few who kept both eyes open, the eye of the soul and the eye of the senses. By sheer devotion to scientific research he discovered the limitations of science two centuries before Einstein and Eddington; but unlike many prophets of the soul, he never disparaged reason in the name of faith, or nature in the name of grace. For him, the material and spiritual universes were joined together by multiple correspondences, and an unbroken chain of discrete degrees."

Hiram Powers, American Sculptor (1805-1873)
"Swedenborg is my author. All other writers (in comparison) seem moving in the dark with tapers in hand, groping their way, while he moves in the broad daylight of the sun."

Edited from the New Church Web site. Accessed 2016:
http://www.newchurch.org/about/swedenborg/influence.html)

For more details and references see also:
Writers Influenced By Swedenborg. Web site accessed 2016:
http://www.swedenborg.org.uk/emanuel_swedenborg/influences

Swedenborg Describes
His Divine Mission and Calling

No ne is born for hell; everyone is born for heaven.
~Swedenborg, HH 329

From my fourth to my tenth year, I was constantly engaged in thought upon God, salvation, and the spiritual sufferings of men, and several times I revealed that at which my father and mother wondered....From my sixth to my twelfth year my delight was to discourse with clergymen concerning Faith-that the life thereof is love, and the love that gives life is the love of one's neighbor. ~Swedenborg, Letters, 1769

At age 57, in the middle of his successful scientific and public career as a mining engineer and publisher of scientific works, Emanuel Swedenborg suddenly found himself conscious in both his natural mind, as we all are, and simultaneously in his spiritual mind, of which we are unconscious until after death. For the next 27 years daily and until his death at age 84, Swedenborg explored the life after death by meeting thousands of people who had lived on earth, some centuries ago, and were now living in a spiritual community in the afterlife of eternity. Swedenborg wrote that the Divine purpose in granting him dual consciousness was to allow him to explore and describe the afterlife of eternity from his perspective as a trained scientist and philosopher. At the same time, Swedenborg's mission was to show how this information about the afterlife is available in the Bible when it is read in its hidden spiritual sense, not just the visible natural and historical sense.

I paste below several selections from Swedenborg's Writings about his Divinely appointed mission or "office" as a revelator. I should explain some of Swedenborg's expressions that he uses throughout his Writings. He referred to his dual consciousness as "the opening of the sight of his spirit". This activation of one's spiritual consciousness normally occurs with everyone when they complete the three-day dying resuscitation procedure. Prior to that, people are functioning in their natural consciousness which is suitable for life on earth through the physical body. At death the physical body is detached and people become conscious in the afterlife world which Swedenborg calls the spiritual world of eternity.

Unlike the normal method Swedenborg became conscious in his spiritual mind even while he was still conscious in his natural mind. Hence it is called "dual citizenship" in relation to consciousness. Swedenborg called this dual capacity the "greatest miracle since creation". Prior to Swedenborg, dozens of prophets and holy people in the Books of the Bible have received the temporary capacity to enter spiritual states of consciousness and to see and hear what was going on there. Immediately afterwards they came back into their natural consciousness and wrote down under inspiration what transpired.

The prophets did not understand the deeper meanings of what they heard and wrote down, and they did not receive the capacity to travel around and interview people in the afterlife. Swedenborg was the only scientist in this history of science and philosophy who has been given this amazing capacity uninterrupted for 27 years. This is why he called it a greater miracle than those witnessed and testified by the prophets of old. Swedenborg saw his Divinely appointed mission as ushering in "the Second Coming of Christ" and thereby completing the formation of the Christian religion established by the Lord when He was on earth. For 17 centuries people have been waiting for the Lord to return as He promised. Swedenborg shows from the spiritual sense of the Bible that the Lord's Second Coming was meant to be a coming or appearance in the minds of people, and not in the physical world.

Here are Swedenborg's various descriptions he gave of his Divinely appointed mission:

That the Lord manifested Himself before me, His servant, and sent me to this office, and that He afterwards opened the sight of my spirit, and so has introduced me into the spiritual world, and has granted me to behold the heavens and the hells and to converse with angels and spirits, and this now uninterruptedly for many years, I testify in truth; likewise, that from the first day of that call I have not received anything that pertains to the doctrines of the New Church from any angel, but from the Lord alone, while I read the Word. (TCR 779)

As, with most in the church at this day, there is no faith in the life after death, and scarcely any [faith] in heaven, or in the Lord [Jesus Christ] as being the God of heaven and earth; therefore the interiors of my spirit have been opened by the Lord, so that I may, while in the [physical] body, be at the same time with the angels in heaven, and not only speak with them, but also see there amazing things, and describe the same; lest perchance hereafter people may say, Who has come to us from heaven, and told us that it exists, and what there is there?

But I know that those who have previously at heart denied a heaven and a hell, and the life after death, will still harden themselves against them, and will deny them; for it is easier to make a raven white, than to cause those to believe who have once at heart rejected faith. But let the things which have thus far been shown concerning heaven and hell and the life after death, be for those few who are in faith. That the rest, however, may be brought to something of acknowledgment, it has been granted that I should relate such things as delight and attract the man who is desirous of having knowledge; and which at present shall be about the earths in the universe. (AC 9439)

A redemption has also been accomplished by the Lord at this day, because the present day is His Second Coming according to prophecy; by which, having been an eye-witness thereof, I have been convinced of the truth of the foregoing arcana. (CORO 21)

The Spirit had been with me from my youth. (Docu. II, p. 187)

After this work was finished the Lord called together His twelve disciples who followed Him in the world; and the next day He sent them all forth throughout the whole spiritual world to preach the Gospel that The Lord God Jesus Christ reigns, whose kingdom shall be for ages and ages, according to the prediction in Daniel (VII, 13, 14), and in the Apocalypse (XI, 15); also that "blessed are they that are called to the marriage supper of the Lamb." (Apoc. XIX, 9). This took place on the nineteenth day of June, 1770.

This is what is meant by these words of the Lord: "He shall send His angels and they shall gather together His elect, from the end of the heavens to the end thereof." (Matthew XXIV, 31) [TCR 709]

Wherefore, in order that true Christian religion might be manifested, it was absolutely necessary that someone should be introduced into the spiritual world, and derive from the mouth of the Lord genuine truths out of the Word. The Lord cannot enlighten anyone with His light, unless He is approached immediately, and acknowledged as the God of heaven. (INV 38)

These things which I saw and heard, I saw and heard in the wakefulness of my body, and at the same time of my spirit; for the Lord has so united my spirit to my body, that I am in both at the same time." (AR 484; cf. CL 1, TCR 851)

The things which I have learned in representations, visions, and from speech with spirits and angels are solely from the Lord .... Thus I have been instructed, consequently by no spirit, nor angel, but by the Lord alone from Whom is everything true and good . . . (SD 1647)

A certain Anglican bishop told how he especially had insulted the five works concerning heaven and hell and the rest which had been presented to all [the bishops] and to all the Protestant lords in the Parliament, vituperating and blaspheming them... Then it was told him that the work is not mine but the Lord's, who desired to reveal the nature of heaven and hell and the quality of the life of man after death and concerning the last judgment... And I also told him that this [revelation] is the male child whom the woman brought forth and whom the dragon wished to devour. [Rev. 12] (SD 6101:2)

That our Savior has visibly revealed Himself before me and commanded [me] to do what I have done and what is yet to be done, and that He thereupon allowed me to come into communion with angels and spirits, I have declared before the whole of Christendom.... That [the Chancellery of Justice now] relates that they still cannot believe it, I cannot take amiss, since I cannot put my state of sight and speech into the heads of others and so convince them, nor can I cause angels and spirits to talk with them; nor is it permitted that miracles should occur nowadays, but reason itself shall find it [true] when with reflection they read my writings in which much is found such as never before has been discovered nor can be discovered without actual sight and conversation with those who are in the spiritual world...

If there should be any further doubt, I am ready to testify with the most solemn oath that may be required of me, that this is [the] truth, complete and actual, without the least fallacy. That our Savior causes this to happen to me is not at all for my sake, but from an urgency which concerns the eternal welfare of all Christians." (Swedenborg's letter to the king, May 25, 1770)

"Read, if you please, the things which have been written in the latest published work, called "The True Christian Religion", concerning the arcana disclosed by the Lord through me His servant... and afterwards draw a conclusion, but from reason, concerning my Revelation." (Swedenborg's letter to Cuno in 1770)

The Lord Jehovah derives and produces from this New Heaven a New Church on the earth, which is done by a Revelation of Truths from His own mouth or from His Word, and by Inspiration. (CORO 18)

When I think of what I am about to write, and while I am writing, I enjoy a complete inspiration, for otherwise it would be my own; but now I know for certain that what I write is the living truth of God." (Swedenborg's testimony as reported by Gjorwell, Doc. II, p. 404)

The Books which were written by the Lord by means of me (a Domino per me), from the beginning to the present day, should be enumerated. (Ecclesiastical History 3)

It has been granted me sometimes to be among the angels of the middle and of the highest heaven, and to hear them conversing with one another; at which time I was in an interior natural state..... I heard things ineffable and inexpressible..... Afterwards it was given me to understand that I could not utter nor describe them by any spiritual and celestial expression, but that nevertheless they could be described even to their rational comprehension by words of natural language. And it was said that there are not any Divine arcana which cannot be perceived and expressed also naturally, although in a more general and imperfect way. (De Verbo 111:4 (6)

From love toward the human race the Lord has made such revelations as will ... conduce to man's salvation. What the Divine has revealed, is with us the Word. (AC 1032)

It has been done in like manner at this day; for it has now pleased the Lord to reveal many arcana of heaven, especially the internal or correspondential sense of the Word, which hitherto has been wholly unknown, and with it He has taught the genuine truths of doctrine; which revelation is meant by the advent of the Lord in Matthew (24: 3, 30, 37) ...In both worlds there is a church, and revelation takes place in both, and through this separation, as also the establishment of a new church. (AE 641)

In place of miracles, there has at this day taken place a manifestation of the Lord Himself, an intromission into the spiritual world, and enlightenment there by means of (per) immediate light from the Lord in such things as are the interior things of the church. But chiefly, the opening of the correspondential sense in the Word, in which the Lord is in His own Divine light. (CORO Mir. IV)

*The manifestation of the Lord in Person, and [my] introduction by the Lord into the spiritual world, both as to sight and as to hearing and speech, **surpasses all miracles**; for we do not read anywhere in history that such intercourse with angels and spirits has been granted from the creation of the world. For I am daily with angels there, even as I am in the world with men; and this now for twenty-seven years. The testimonies of this intercourse are the books which have been published by me concerning heaven and hell, and also the memorable relations thence in the last work, called the True Christian Religion ... Tell me, who ever before has known anything about heaven and hell, about the state of man after death, about spirits and angels, etc., etc. (INV 43, 44)*

*Besides these most evident testimonies [there is the fact] that the correspondential sense of the Word has been disclosed by the Lord through me, which **has never before been revealed** since the Word was written among the sons of Israel; and this (hie) is the very Sanctuary of the Word: The Lord Himself is in this [sense] with His Divine, and in the natural sense with His Human. This, even as to an iota, cannot be opened except by the Lord Himself. This surpasses all the revelations which have been made since the creation of the world. Through this revelation there is opened a communication of men with the angels of heaven, and a conjunction of the two worlds has been effected; since when man is in the natural sense, the angels are in the correspondential sense. (INV 43, 44)*

*The manifestation of the Lord and intromission into the spiritual world, surpass all miracles. This **has not been granted to any one since the creation** as it has been to me. The men of the Golden Age indeed spoke with angels, but it was not granted them to be in any other than natural light; but to me it is granted to be in both spiritual and natural light at the same time. By this means it has been granted me to see the wonderful things of heaven, to be together with the angels as one of them, and at the same time to draw forth (haurire) truths in light and thus to perceive and teach them; consequently to be led by the Lord. (INV 52)*

This Second Advent of the Lord is effected by means of a man before whom He has manifested Himself in Person and whom He has filled with His Spirit, to teach the doctrines of the New Church through the Word from Him. " ...It follows that He is to do it by means of a man, who is able not only to receive the doctrines of this Church with his understanding, but also to publish them by the press. That the Lord has manifested Himself before me His servant and sent me on this office, and that, after this, He opened the sight of my spirit and thus let me into the spiritual world and gave me to see the heavens and the hells, and also to speak with angels and spirits, and this now for many years, I testify in truth; and also that from the first day of that call, I have not received any thing which pertains to the doctrines of that Church from any angel, but from the Lord alone while I read the Word. (TCR 779)

The doctrine of the church is that this is the Advent of the Lord and that thence it is that arcana have been opened by the Lord respecting heaven and hell, man's life after death, the Word, the last judgment- which have all been written out in Latin and sent to all the archbishops and bishops of the kingdom [of Great Britain] and to the nobility. And still not a word has been heard, a sign that they do not interiorly care for the things of heaven and the church, and that it is now the very end of the church and indeed that the church no longer exists. (Concerning the Athanasian Creed 2)

Without the advent of the Lord into the world, no one could have been saved. It is similar at this day: wherefore unless the Lord came again into the world in Divine truth which is the Word, not any one can be saved. (True Christian Religion 3)

My opinion is that we are not to judge Swedenborg's Writings merely by reading his claims (as given in the selections above), but by carefully studying and researching his 30 volumes, noting carefully whether there are inconsistencies or incomplete justifications. I have been engaged in this serious study for the past 35 years using my trained skills in scientific theory and history. I found no inconsistency and no lack of rational and empirical justification to all the claims and principles that Swedenborg formulated. Any person can do this for oneself. I recommend that people read Swedenborg directly, and only afterwards to read how others have interpreted his ideas. Three of his books that I suggest would be good to start with are: Divine Providence (DP); Heaven and Hell (HH); Conjugial Love (CL).

All Swedenborg books are available online full text and free at the *Internet Sacred Texts Archive*: http://www.sacred-texts.com/swd/index.htm

Swedenborg Books and Resources on the Web

All of Swedenborg's Writings full text, free, and searchable online:
http://www.heavenlydoctrines.org/

Internet Sacred Texts Archive (all Swedenborg books full text and free):
http://www.sacred-texts.com/swd/index.htm

Swedenborg: The Divine Revelation of the New Jerusalem. Expanded Edition compiled by T. Webber (2012). (30 volumes of Swedenborg collected in one digital Kindle Edition at a reasonable price).

Tafel, R. L. (1890). *Documents Concerning the Life and Character of Emanuel Swedenborg* (standard reference source and authoritative documentation):
http://swedenborgdigitallibrary.org/tafel/tafeltc.html

Swedenborg: Buddha of the North by D. T. Suzuki (1996) (the famous Zen Buddhist scholar shows Swedenborg's ideas compatible with Buddhism):
http://ccbs.ntu.edu.tw/FULLTEXT/JR-PHIL/ew94208.htm

The Swedenborg Digital Library (full text and free; also collateral works)
http://www.swedenborgdigitallibrary.org/index.html

The Swedenborg Epic. The Life and Works of Emanuel Swedenborg by C. Sigstedt (impartial and thorough presentation of Swedenborg's life, reputation, and principal ideas):
http://www.swedenborgdigitallibrary.org/ES/epictc.htm

Wikipedia: Emanuel Swedenborg Entry (general summary, references, and links):
https://en.wikipedia.org/wiki/Emanuel_Swedenborg

The Gist of Swedenborg (brief selections on various topics):
http://amzn.to/1Q6b0ZD

Emanuel Swedenborg: Visionary Savant in the Age of Reason by Ernst Benz (classic biography focusing on Swedenborg's mental states and emotional life):
http://www.swedenborg.com/product/emanuel-swedenborg/

A Scientist Explores Spirit (short introduction to Swedenborg's life and an overview of key concepts)
http://www.swedenborg.com/product/a-scientist-explores-spirit/
http://www.swedenborg.com/product/essays-nce/

The Swedenborg YouTube Channel:
https://www.youtube.com/user/offTheLeftEye

The Swedenborg Foundation: Publisher of the works of Swedenborg and collateral books and videos.
http://www.swedenborg.com/

The New Church Organization and Library:
http://www.newchurch.org/
http://www.brynathyn.edu/

The Path: the Inner Life of Jesus Christ (presentation based on Swedenborg's exegesis of the Old Testament):
http://amzn.to/1Py2kp3

Online Books on Theistic Psychology by Leon James (free and full text)
http://www.theisticpsychology.org/resources.htm

Online books on Jung and Swedenborg by Leon James:
http://amzn.to/1XeFkAD

END OF CHAPTER 2

Chapter 3
Jung on Dreams and
the Psychic World

My dreams, are the speech of my soul. Dreams are the guiding words of the soul. Dreams pave the way for life, and they determine you without you understanding their language. ~Carl Jung, The Red Book, 233

We also live in our dreams; we do not live only by day. Sometimes we accomplish our greatest deeds in dreams. ~Carl Jung, The Red Book, p. 242

Dreams have influenced all the important changes in my life and theories. ~Carl Jung, 1925 Seminar, Lecture 3, p. 15-26

Dreams are the guiding words of the soul. ~Carl Jung

No one can become conscious of the shadow without considerable moral effort. To become conscious of it involves recognizing the dark aspects of the personality as present and real. ~Carl Jung, Aion

The Spiritual Reality of the Psychic World

Freud had a perspective on dreams that saw them from the outside after the fact, as reported or remembered later by the patient. As presented in his 1900 book *The Interpretation of Dreams* in which Freud described his approach to dream analysis that introduced psychological meaning in terms of hidden symbolism that was motivated by the patient's psychodynamics of emotional repression. This psychological approach to dream interpretation was guided by pre-established concepts from Freud's psychoanalytic system of thinking. Psychoanalytic dream interpretation was highly successful and widely accepted by psychiatrists and introduced as themes into novels, film, and magazines. It was also acclaimed by many dedicated followers and has continued the life and use of psychoanalysis for more than a century.

Jung's perspective on dreams was of an entirely different sort. The two approaches stand in sharp and opposite relation to dualism. Freud's approach to dreams is a materialistic application, while Jung's definition of dreams is dualist. Jung's idea of what are dreams is deeper and more objective since the archetypes that caused dreams were collective, universal, and anatomical or biological, and therefore objective and empirical, unlike Freud's dream analysis that may be called subjective and hypothetical. Freud looked at the consequent effects in dreaming, which were merely so many detailed external appearances in which dreams were cast, while Jung looked at the cause of the dream, which is its interior objective psychic origin.

Freud also discussed dreams as being psychological expressions caused by the dreamer's desire to hide elements of the self that were too threatening to conscious awareness. Wrapping dreams into layers of distractions was viewed as a defense mechanism that the patient was using to repress certain emotions and feelings that were simply unacceptable to the conscious ego. These emotions and feelings were real and were part of everyone's biological system of needs. Hence repressing them from the conscious ego resulted in displacement and neurotic or inappropriate ways of expressing them. Freudian therapy involved bringing these repressed or "unconscious" realities about oneself into the conscious and integrating them into the personality.

Jung added a totally independent dimension to dreams that gave them objective existence in another world called the "psychic" world. Freud denied the independent existence of a psychic world since he was a scientific materialist in which mind is purely physical and is part of the biology of the *physical* brain. This monistic view of the mind is still in effect today in neuroscience and materialistic psychology. There is discussion today in neuroscience that mind and consciousness may be "emergent" phenomena but these are still physical and have no independent existence from the physical brain. Hence at death or in a coma the mind does not emerge or exist.

But Jung was a scientific dualist who formulated psychological theory in terms of the mind's own nature that was independent of the physical brain. The laws of biology in the psychic world were not the same as those in the physical world. Hence all mental activity existed not from or in the physical brain, but from and in the psychic world where nothing physical could exist. Therefore ordinary cause-effect relations operating in the physical world were entirely different in the psychic world.

For example, in materialistic psychology everything we know or think of must originate from things we have learned or experienced in interaction with physical things or social events. All ideas that appeared new were in fact transformations of old ideas that were learned. This transformation process was called creativity. But in dualist psychology, there exist biologically universal ideas that have a completely independent origin and existence from the individual and the physical world. When Jung formulated this approach to the psychic world Freud rejected it and broke his support and contact with Jung. After that split, the two giants of psychology took complete separate and opposed courses of development and application. Today Freudians and Jungians are at opposite ends of psychological systems, although it is fair to say that this view is not shared by some analysts.

Jung came to the realization that when we recognize this independent existence of the archetypes, we empower ourselves to discover and understand what lies within ourselves. Although Freud wrote that dreams are the "*royal road to the unconscious*" it is only through the work of Jung that we can come to discover what lies in the unconscious. Dreams offer us knowledge about human beings and guidance about God that was also known to the ancients. Dreams have their own life and purpose in the human psyche. They are according to Jung "*a spontaneous self-portrayal in symbolic form of the actual situation in the unconscious*".

Jung held that the unconscious is informing the individual through the dream. The personality always progresses towards greater individuation and potential fulfillment. The unconscious helps this process in various ways, and one is to present a dream that informs the individual of some important inner element that is part of the future state of the personality. We can then incorporate these new elements into our changing personality. The dream is the larger Self talking to the narrower ego. Unlike Freud who held that dreams are hidden or have latent meaning, Jung states that dreams do not "disguise or distort", nor "deceive or lie", but present the unvarnished truth about the individual.

But there is a difficulty in hearing clearly the voice of the dream because it is complex and speaks in symbolic images of universal archetypes. Dreams are applied simultaneously to several levels of the personality and can present difficulty of interpretation. The lower or external level of the dream is merely a dramatic event that we recall as the dream. This is the "objective level". A second level called the "subjective level" applies the dream content to the individual who has the dream. The various characters in the dream become representatives of the individual's particular characteristics. A third level is the application to the individual of some archetype that is operative in the individual's unconscious.

Dreams pave the way for life, and they determine you without your understanding their language. ~Carl Jung, The Red Book, p. 233

Dreams are natural biological objects that are wrapped in multiple anatomical layers that can be gradually unfolded and comprehended over a period of years. A dream develops and deepens as we interact with it on a long-term basis.

"Dreams are impartial, spontaneous products of the unconscious psyche, outside the control of the will. They are pure nature; they show us the unvarnished, natural truth, and are therefore fitted, as nothing else is, to give us back an attitude that accords with our basic human nature when our consciousness has strayed too far from its foundations and run into an impasse. ~Carl Jung, C.W., 10, par. 317

I present here various brief selections on dreams from Jung's work.

The basis of Jungian analysis is the psychodynamic by which portions of the collective unconscious become conscious to one's ego. This process goes on throughout one's life but accelerates as we get older and closer to making our transition to our next life. Viewed superficially this statement sounds like it is as true of Freud as it is of Jung. The only difference seems to be that Freud recognized the "unconscious" but denied the "collective unconscious" as being really different. This seemingly little difference between "unconscious" and "collective unconscious" is however similar to the difference between earth and sky. If you had to fly over the ocean with an earthbound vehicle you would never make it. Earth is real and requires a real vehicle riding over the ground. The sky is real and requires a flying vehicle such as an airplane, rocket, or wind carried construction like wings, balloons, or parasails. While Jung acknowledges both earthbound and flying vehicles, Freud denies the possibility of flying vehicles.

Entirely different and opposed conclusions are involved. Jung explored and discovered the objects and properties of the independent psychic world such as the collective unconscious and archetypes. These formed a biological part of every human being since the beginning of the race. Jungian depth psychology was therefore defined as the interaction between the independent collective unconscious and the individual mind and personality. Every psychological phenomenon involved this connection. Nothing psychological could exist separately from this interconnection.

Psychology does not exist without the psychic world. Our personality, ego, or self exist within the psychic world. Consciousness draws its existence and function from the psychic world. All things in the psychic world are independent of physical matter, physical time, and physical space. Our feelings, thoughts and perceptions exist independently of physical matter, time, and space. This means that when we are born our mind is not in the same world as the physical brain or body. Once we become a person with thoughts and feelings we have these independently of the physical body.

Hence when the physical body dies, the connection between our personality and the physical world is broken. We then live our existence exclusively through interaction with the psychic world. Our personality is consequently immortal since the beginning. From literature we know that modern people have been searching for the secret to immortality for centuries. They did not know that we are born immortal. Their search had no meaning and missed reality. Of course ancient civilizations knew of immortality, but modern science in the materialistic mode forgot about it and denied it.

In the history of psychology and in psychology courses taught today in high school and college, the name of Descartes is most often associated with "dualism". In neuroscience literature Descartes dualism is rejected as unscientific because he separated mind from the physical body. The argument is that a "disembodied mind" is not a scientific concept. This would be true if only the physical body existed at birth. But if the psychic world is independent of the physical then our mind exists not in this world but in the psychic world. Descartes did not discuss the independent psychic world that Jung discussed and described. Two centuries before Jung, Swedenborg was also a scientific dualist. Both Jung and Swedenborg went further than Descartes by describing the mind-body that we acquired at birth.

To formulate a scientific theory of the immortal mind it is necessary to describe the mind or personality as psychic operations in a human mind-body. We could not have a stable and permanent mental system of operation like that of an individual's personality, existing in nothing or in mere psychic space flitting about like a ghost perhaps. This would not be scientific. Hence the challenge for scientific dualism was to describe the anatomy of the mind-body. This means that we are born with two bodies, not just one.

The physical body contains the physical brain and all the organs of sensory perception and motor operation. The mind-body or psychic body is born simultaneously in the psychic world. The two bodies function together in total synchrony. The physical body is functionally related to the psychic body so that we have voluntary movement in the physical body. This means that the mind in its psychic body, which is the person or ego, is able to control the voluntary movements of the physical body as it wishes.

Today we can think of virtual reality and avatars that we learn to control in movement. The physical body is therefore the avatar of the psychic body through which we can perceive and move around in a physical world. Without this physical body or avatar we would not be able to perceive and function in the physical world. When this temporary avatar no longer functions or is said to "die", we are completely cut off from the physical world. At that point our psychic body is no longer limited to perception and movement through the physical avatar. The connection is broken forever. Now we receive all our sensory input and motor operations through our psychic body only.

Until that point of cut-off or "death" our conscious life in the ego was completely restricted to the input from the physical avatar. This connection was so strong and exclusive that all we normally knew consciously was the physical world around the avatar. We were completely unconscious to the psychic world around our psychic body. We were in effect monists, like the materialist scientists. We could even deny the existence of the psychic body and world.

But when the "death" separation occurs we can no longer receive any input from the physical world. All of a sudden, the moment the avatar stops functioning, we become fully conscious of the psychic world around us. What an amazing moment that must be when we suddenly awaken, as if from sleep, and gain control over the psychic body. All of a sudden we can see the people and objects in the psychic world. We can talk with and touch the people who have "died" before us from the beginning of humanity. We can experience a new life of wonder that follows the rules of this new world. Very quickly we forget all about the "former life" in the avatar. We are now in a realm that is truly suited for human life to develop and evolve. Social relationships now function differently, very differently, and our day-to-day living proceeds in very different ways.

Most significantly for psychology, Jung and Swedenborg described the synchronous relationship between the ever-present collective unconscious and the developing ego personality. Our ego-consciousness is a base experience for each of us human beings. This ego-consciousness is nothing but our self-awareness as a unique identify or individual, distinct from all other existing individuals. This ego is of course a psychic operation or organ-system that is constantly going on within our unique psychic body. Our individual ego is like a tree, never ceasing to grow, being constantly active from within, moment-by-moment, while we are awake or asleep. There must be a constant circulation of psychic nourishment for this mind-body.

For instance, if you sit quietly relaxed and without doing anything else, you become immediately aware of the continuous stream of thoughts and accompanying emotions that fill your conscious awareness. This is the ego being fed through continuous experiencing. We know where the food comes from for the tree or grass in our yard. But what about the food for the mind, one wonders, where is that coming from. The thoughts and emotions that are endlessly streaming across our experience and awareness are being consumed by our affective and cognitive systems in the immortal mind-body. This is the growth of our mental anatomy, which collectively is called ego.

From a helpless infant we become a child and then a teenager. Consider what is the flesh of this rapid growth of our personality from simple and basic, to more and more complex as our mind becomes a mature adult. We know more words and meanings. We learn to comprehend more complex social ideas and skills in reasoning. We enlarge our capacity to control our environment, to love or to despise others, to be honest or to cheat, to be obedient to conscience or to repress it, to acknowledge God or to deny. This is the "inner freedom" through which our personality grows and matures as our psychic body.

Further, consider the importance for a tree of the environment; both distant like the climate of the region, and proximal, like the sphere of air and temperature immediately around the tree, and the compact sphere of the ground that surrounds the roots. Similarly, psychic spheres that surround our psychic body greatly influence our ego and personality development through the nature and quality of the psychic food that is inhaled and in which it is completely immersed.

The anatomy of our immortal psychic body is the anatomy of the mind. Its organ systems are not composed of material substance like the physical body but of psychic substance that is exists plentifully throughout the atmospheres of the psychic world. We can understand the nature of the psychic world by realizing that dreams occur in the psychic world and not in the physical world. When we dream our mind effortlessly constructs detailed and complex scenery in which the objects and characters have virtually the same appearance as the objects and people we perceive through our physical avatar.

In the physical world it takes much effort and expertise on the part of a team of people to construct a film studio or stage set in which physical avatars can move around and be active in their character role. But in the psychic world this whole process is effortless and instantaneous. The methods of constructing in the two worlds are entirely different. One striking contrast is how we deal with psychic space and psychic time in dreams or in imagination. In our dream sequence psychic space as we move around is instantaneously constructed as needed. We never have to run out of space if we don't want to. Similarly, we don't need money or construction materials to create our dream objects. Psychic time is created to be short or long, as we wish it to be. We can as easily travel billions of miles in an instant as we take a single step. We can time travel back or forward in our psychic calendar.

Many people educated in the modern era have acquired an ego personality whose thoughts and reasoning are immersed in nothing but natural consciousness. We are taught materialistic ideas with which to think and function as a citizen. We hear others talk about the spiritual world and life after death but we hardly can believe that there is such a thing. Even those who adopt a religious outlook understand it naturally not spiritually.

For instance, in thinking about life after death they think that the "resurrection from death" is going to be from the grave back into the physical world with their former or new physical body that they will miraculously receive again as they had before. People are unable or unwilling to think of life after death that is not in a physical world. When we are immersed in our ego in this purely natural consciousness we think of our dreams and imagination as "fantasy" and "not really real". We are unable or unwilling to let our consciousness rise above the physical nature and into the psychic nature. But when we do, we are able to think of dreams as substantial and real, more real in fact than the material objects that are merely physical and therefore temporary, not really real.

If we accept the description of the psychic or spiritual world as objectively experienced by Jung and Swedenborg, our ego suddenly enters the sphere of spiritual consciousness and understanding. We become capable of thinking and reasoning with spiritual rationality that is a level higher than natural rationality and thinking. The psychic world makes rational sense when we operate in spiritual consciousness. It is obvious that we must be born with an immortal psychic body that functions anatomically through mental nourishment and growth. It is obvious that an all powerful human God is at the center of everything that exists and is going on.

Those who read Jung and attempt to think about the collective unconscious are often faced with a frightening experience that makes them draw back rather than enter. The discovery of the "shadow" archetype becomes a menacing and dangerous mental trip. Scary characters appear in our consciousness and disappear. We think of becoming mad or insane. We brace ourselves trying to hold on to sanity and rational order. This is the experiencing of the psychic world alone and unprotected by God's loving hand. But the instant we acknowledge God's co-presence and omnipresence we are back in reality and the frightening cold of the collective unconscious melts away and in its place there is the reassuring warmth of love and rational comprehension.

One might wonder for instance about the characters we encounter in our dreams and imagination. Are they real people? We can now provide an empirical answer to this puzzle when we combine the experiences of Jung in the psychic world and the experiences of Swedenborg in the spiritual world. "Psychic" and "spiritual" both have to do with what is mental. Hence we can take three expressions as equivalent in reference: the psychic world, the spiritual world, and the mental world. They all refer to the same reality. This is similar to the reference we make to the physical world, the natural world, and the material world. These are the same.

So the dualist contrast in science is either to refer to the material world as the only reality, a position known as monism, or to refer to reality as consisting of two independent worlds one physical or natural, the other spiritual or psychic. That these two worlds are "independent" means that their nature is entirely different and distinct, each having their own existence and laws of operation.

In the physical world gravity and energy are the effective operators of events. In the psychic world, spiritual love is the strongest operative force. After that comes spiritual rationality or spiritual truth. Spiritual love and spiritual truth powerfully and intensely seek each other in order to unite again as they are in the mind of God. This is the mechanism or biological operation by which God elevates the individual's level of consciousness from natural to spiritual. Among the ancients who knew all these things I write about, this elevation procedure was called *rebirth* and also *spiritual birth*.

In religious symbolism, spiritual birth is called *creation of man*. The person who remained in natural consciousness was called a *dead man*. Hence to "*create man*" and to thus be "*be reborn*", refers to the process of becoming spiritual through regeneration of character from selfish to mutual love. This critical psychotherapeutic process is discussed throughout this book. Everyone is born with an inherited and powerful love for self and to make the self to be dominant over everyone else so that we can exploit them for our own sake. This is a deadly selfishness when considered spiritually.

As we grow older and become adults we have a fateful spiritual choice to make. We can continue the path of selfishness and erect our entire personality and love immersed in it, or we can have an about face and journey in the other direction. This is the spiritual awakening from the deadly coma of selfishness to the light and warmth of mutual love and love of God. Once this turnabout has been made with the acknowledgement of God's role in our mind, we are undergoing the lifelong discipline of regeneration or individuation, as will be discussed throughout this book.

> *You see, life wants to be real; if you love life you want to*
> *live really, not as a mere promise hovering above things.*
> *~Carl Jung, Zarathustra Seminar, p. 508*

Spiritual awakening is powerfully active in the psychic world from the power of spiritual love. Even if our psychic body is riddled with selfish organic structures yet spiritual love is powerful enough to heal its organic structures. We can become more conscious of such psychic influences if we pay attention to the correspondences that we learn from language and talk.

Both Jung and Swedenborg cautioned that human beings are like animals when they function in natural or materialistic consciousness prior to synchronous activation from the spiritual mind that is located within or above the natural mind.

This materialistic or natural level of thinking in psychology has been the standard throughout the 20th century and is exemplified in the history of psychology seen in the works of Sigmund Freud and B. F. Skinner. I think it is a historical irony that the followers of Skinner accused the followers of Freud of using bogus science. Freud believed and insisted that his psychology was strictly scientific.

Either way, the psychology of both Skinner and Freud is purely materialistic, denying dualism, denying the psychic world as an independently existing environment, denying spirituality, denying life after death, denying God and God's active role in every activity.

We could not possibly judge this world if we had not also a standpoint outside, and that is given by the symbolism of religious experiences. ~Carl Jung, Kundalini Seminar, p. 27

Jung and Swedenborg stand in sharp contrast to Freud and Skinner. For both Jung and Swedenborg, God was not only real but was the center of their lives. As psychologists, they both had a strong preference for the empirical and scientific method. Their explanations were systematic and data-based. Their central concepts included:

- an independent psychic world
- God's active involvement with the individual
- life after death and immortality of the personality
- heaven and hell as mental states in every individual
- the psychic or spiritual world of the afterlife in eternity
- the psychic world of the collective unconscious
- the universal validity of religious symbolisms, myths, and dreams.

Each of these concepts would have been denied by Freud and Skinner and rejected by them as not-science. And yet everyone can see that all these concepts were experientially observed and empirically discovered, not subjectively hypothesized or invented. Both Jung and Swedenborg experienced the other world directly and were able to talk to the people who had passed into the afterlife. This is objective evidence-based description.

I should mention that Jung had only sporadic and brief visits in the psychic world of the collective unconscious lasting a few minutes or hours at a time. Swedenborg had dual consciousness for 27 continuous years on a 24/7 basis. This explains why we find almost no details in Jung's work of the people and communities in the afterlife, while in Swedenborg we find a detailed ethnography of interviews of the people in the afterlife, also a mental geography of their location and communication patterns with each other, and various psychological experiments that can only be carried out in the psychic world.

More details about our immortal "afterlife" is presented below and throughout this book.

The immortality of our ego or personality comes from the fact that the psychic world is not part of the time-space continuum that is familiar to us while we are attached to our physical world. As we know from Swedenborg's work, the three-day dying-resuscitation process separates us from our physical body, and consequently from all input from the physical world.

What is unconscious and frightening in our mind is represented by *the shadow* archetype. In order to develop psychologically to a state of wholeness, the individual needs to wrestle with the shadow, to acknowledge its reality as part of ourselves.

Wholeness Requires That We Are To Know Ourselves

Self-knowledge is not possible without confronting and vanquishing the shadow.

This activity may take years to progress and complete due to the resistance we put up to the growth process. Volume 2 of this book presents a spiritual discipline that is titled "rational theistic self-analysis" (RTS) in which I recapitulate the main themes of this volume that focuses more intensely on the work of Jung and Swedenborg. RTS is a practical application of their work adapted to the new millennium.

I predict that in the next few decades science will begin to incorporate more and more concepts from theistic scientific dualism. It will thereby greatly enlarge its ability to help meet the spiritual needs of humanity. One of these is to assist people in regeneration or individuation, which not only makes them happier and more productive individuals, but also equips their personality with traits that can thrive in the heavenly regions of the afterlife.

The human psyche existed before the individual ego was born.

> *The meaning of events is the way of salvation that you create. The meaning of events comes from the possibility of life in this world that you create. It is the mastery of this world and the assertion of your soul in this world. ~Carl Jung, The Red Book, p. 239*

All of humanity's memories and secrets are located in the collective unconscious.

Our mental health requires that we recover and garner from this dark expanse of mental forces, that which is our Self. The pieces of our ego belonging to the Self are scattered in the mysterious unfathomable expanse of the dark psyche.

Our task in this world is to individuate, which is to find and collect the pieces of our self found in the collective unconscious, and to introduce them to our conscious, in order that we may know them and integrate them into our personality for the sake of achieving wholeness.

Analyzing our dreams is a form of self-analysis. It helps us in this task of reconstructing the scattered self into a coherent whole again.

> *The dream is a little hidden door in the innermost and most secret recesses of the soul, opening into that cosmic night which was psyche long before there was any ego-consciousness, and which will remain psyche no matter how far our ego-consciousness extends. ~Carl Jung, Memories Dreams and Reflections.*

According to Jung the characters that we read about in literary works may be viewed as "*representatives of relatively autonomous functional complexes in the psyche of the author*" (Jung, *Definitions*). Swedenborg makes a similar point about the characters that are mentioned in *Sacred Scripture* such as Moses, Joshua, Samson, Job, King Nebuchadnezzar,

King David, the Dragon, the woman clothed with the sun, with the moon under her feet, and so on.

These historical and mythical characters are mentioned in God's Word because they each represent some psychological complex in human beings who are undergoing the process of individuation through regeneration or character reformation. Swedenborg demonstrates that figuring out the correspondential meaning of Sacred Scripture yields a divine anatomical handbook of the human mind. In other words, *the spiritual meaning of Sacred Scripture constitutes the foundation of rational theistic psychology.* And this refers to the Sacred Scripture of all the major religions, as they all have the same spiritual information through correspondences. This extracted spiritual information, which is universal and scientific, is completely independent of the literal-historical meaning, which is localized and forms the basis of the cultural and historical religions of the past few thousand years.

The unraveling of spiritual representations helps us to know our psychic context. This is a necessary psychological growth task that we must perform. As Jung says, "*By understanding the unconscious we free ourselves from its domination*".

Jung says that knowing our dreams is the way God speaks to us. Without this knowledge, our consciousness "*strays too far from its foundations and runs into an impasse*".

According to Jung the unconscious "*contains everything that is lacking in the conscious*" and therefore it has a "*compensatory*" function of essential function in the growth process of becoming whole and well.

> *It is impossible to live as an ego forever, it is too childish. Of course, many people often make the mistake of taking the ego for the Self. The ego is nothing but the artificial self. ~Carl Jung, Visions Seminar, p. 369*

Jung uses the expression the "artificial self" in a pejorative sense that this self is a fake. It is "childish". It is not the "real self" that is actually the constituent of our mind and Self. The fake self is all that the ego is made of. Ego-consciousness is ignorant of its own insignificance and non-existence.

In Swedenborg the artificial or illusory self is called the "proprium", which is Latin for "own" or "ego". Swedenborg describes the proprium as evil, ugly and selfish to the extreme. It is not merely artificial or self-constructed, but evil, spiteful, and spreading corruption. Jung calls it a "*lower level of personality*" in which we behave "*like a primitive*".

No one escapes the lower psychic states of ego-consciousness. Therefore it is a phase of growth that must change and adapt. This process of change involves the central features of the personality since these have been corrupted by the attacks of the shadow. Hence the process of psychological adaptation is emotionally painful and psychologically stressful.

Emotion is not an activity of the individual but something that happens to him . ~Carl Jung, Aion

If you are not interested in your own fate, the unconscious is. ~Carl Jung, 1958, Talk With Students

In sleep, fantasy takes the form of dreams. But in waking life, too, we continue to dream beneath the threshold of consciousness, especially when under the influence of repressed or other unconscious complexes. ~Carl Jung, Problems of Modern Self-analysis, 1929

Looking Through the Window to the Unconscious

Jung clearly recognizes that our emotional life is dominated by the shadow in our unconscious. This is at the beginning, when we experience emotions as "*something that happens*" to us. We thus recognize that our emotional life is still primitive, belonging to our "*lower level of personality*". In that ego state we are not in control but feel controlled, like a "*passive victim*". In a primitive mental state we are "*incapable of moral judgment*".

Jung wrote about the shadow:

> *The shadow is a moral problem that challenges the whole ego-personality....., for no one can become conscious of the shadow without considerable moral effort. To become conscious of it involves recognizing the dark aspects of the personality as present and real. This act is the essential condition for any kind of self-knowledge, and it therefore, as a rule, meets with considerable resistance. Indeed, self-knowledge as a psycho-therapeutic measure frequently requires much painstaking work extending over a long period.*

> *Closer examination of the dark characteristics that is, the inferiorities constituting the shadow reveals that they have an emotional nature, a kind of autonomy, and accordingly an obsessive or, better, possessive quality.*

> *Emotion, incidentally, is not an activity of the individual but something that happens to him. Affects occur usually where adaptation is weakest, and at the same time they reveal the reason for its weakness, namely a certain degree of inferiority and the existence of a lower level of personality. On this lower level with its uncontrolled or scarcely controlled emotions one behaves more or less like a primitive, who is not only the passive victim of his affects but also singularly incapable of moral judgment. ~Carl Jung, Aion*

To face and manage the shadow, as everyone must, we are required to put up "*considerable moral effort*". It is a "psycho-therapeutic" measure by which we are made to "*face our inferiorities*". It requires "*self-knowledge*" and the motivation to overcome the "*resistance*" we feel when we face the "*dark aspects of the personality*". This is precisely the therapeutic function of dreams, namely, to open up the windows of perception into their symbolic meaning and psychological significance.

A dream is a hidden door to deeper layers that affect the personality. The psychic forces in the collective unconscious wish to re-enter the conscious ego. These living human psychic forces speak to our conscious ego in a figurative language that is produced in our individual mind by the laws of universal symbolism. Swedenborg called this universal activity as the "laws of correspondence" between all natural things and spiritual things.

Correspondences are universal biological laws that transform the unconscious spiritual nature of the psychic forces into natural activity that corresponds to it. This is the content of the dream that we remember. The events and details of our dreams consist of natural things such as we find in our daily waking lives here on earth. These natural events and objects are produced in our dream by the transformation from spiritual to natural meaning or consciousness. In the dream there is to be found the spiritual that is within the natural, or the collective unconscious that is within the individual conscious.

Jung argued therefore that to take dreams "literally" is to miss their psychological significance, which can be obtained only by figuring out its symbolic meaning. The same principle is at work in "*literary works*" where the characters represent "*functional complexes in the psyche of the author*".

Jung writes:

> *The dream is a little hidden door in the innermost and most secret recesses of the soul, opening into that cosmic night which was psyche long before there was any ego-consciousness, and which will remain psyche no*

matter how far our ego-consciousness extends. ~Carl Jung, Memories Dreams and Reflections

As most people know, one of the basic principles of analytical psychology is that dream-images are to be understood symbolically; that is to say, one must not take them literally, but must surmise a hidden meaning in them. ~Carl Jung, Symbols of Transformation, para. 4

Interpretation on the subjective level allows us to take a broader psychological view not only of dreams but also of literary works, in which the individual figures then appear as representatives of relatively autonomous functional complexes in the psyche of the author. ~Carl Jung, Definitions, CW 6, par. 813

He whose desire turns away from outer things, reaches the place of the soul. ~Carl Jung, The Red Book, p. 233.

By understanding the unconscious we free ourselves from its domination. ~ Carl Jung, Memories, Dreams, Reflections

We must begin to learn about man until every Jekyll can see his Hyde. ~Carl Jung, C.G. Jung Speaking: Interviews and Encounters, p. 244-251

And you can be sure that the dream is your nearest friend; the dream is the friend of those who are not guided any more by the traditional truth and in consequence are isolated. ~Carl Jung, CW 18, Para 674

What we need is the development of the inner spiritual man, the unique individual whose treasure is hidden on the one hand in the symbols of our mythological tradition, and on the other hand in man's unconscious psyche. ~Carl Jung, Letters Vol. II, p. 201-208

We have forgotten the age-old fact that God speaks chiefly through dreams and visions. ~Carl Jung, Man and His Symbols, 1964

Besides the obvious personal sources, creative fantasy also draws upon the forgotten and long buried primitive mind with its host of images, which are to be found in the mythologies of all ages and all peoples. ~Carl Jung, CW 5, Pages xxiv-xxv

To dream is to produce a performance. One becomes the author of the dream drama. A dream is actually a literary production, a work of art in which the characters, objects, and tones represent the psychological complexes of the individual.

The dream is a map of the state of the unconscious in relation to ego-consciousness. By getting to know and to understand this map we "*free ourselves from the domination*" of the unconscious. We become more individuated, "more unique" as a person, more of who we really are, undistorted by convention and illusion. This is our "*spiritual man*" in which lies our spiritual consciousness, where the collective unconscious is no longer hostile and uncooperative. This is where and when we have access to the larger and true Self that uniquely exists for each individual in the collective unconscious of humanity.

In our spiritual consciousness we are in touch with God who "*speaks chiefly through dreams and visions*". I will show in the next Chapter that presents Swedenborg that God uses this same language of symbolism or correspondence in all Sacred Scripture.

Jung stated that "*the shadow is a moral problem*". He was referring to the emotional conflict and dilemmas that we experience when the "*dark aspects of the personality*" are given an entry point into our conscious awareness. In order to attain "*any kind of self-knowledge*" we have no choice but to compel ourselves to look at what lies within the depth of our own mind and that of the human mind. This is not something that we create. It is within us, within our personality, by human birth. This psychic depth has sometimes been called the "*cosmic night*" and the "deep sea".

In the self good and evil are indeed closer than identical twins!
~Carl Jung, CW 12, Para 24

If you are dishonest, you are nothing for your unconscious.
~Carl Jung, C.G. Jung Speaking: Interviews and Encounters, p. 359-364

Jung states that emotions have "*a kind of autonomy*": "*Emotion is not an activity of the individual but something that happens to him*". Our personality functions at a lower and a higher level simultaneously. The lower level experiences emotions in the raw, as it were, so that we do not have a rational level of thinking to mitigate the obsessive-compulsive nature of emotions. At this lower level of personality functioning our emotions are "*scarcely controlled*" and we are incapable of moral judgment.

Most people confuse "self-knowledge" with knowledge of their conscious ego personalities. Anyone who has any ego-consciousness at all takes it for granted that he knows himself. But the ego knows only its own contents, not the unconscious and its contents. People measure their self-knowledge by what the average person in their social environment knows of himself, but not by the real psychic facts which are for the most part hidden from them. In this respect the psyche behaves like the body, of whose physiological and anatomical structure the average person knows very little too. Although he lives in it and with it, most of it is totally unknown to the layman, and special scientific knowledge is needed to acquaint consciousness with what is known of the body, not to speak of all that is not known, which also exists. ~Carl Jung, The Undiscovered Self*

Jung taught that self-knowledge is a "psycho-therapeutic" healing process that goes on for a lifetime. The dream is the "*inner door*" that allows some meaning to cross over from the unconscious to the conscious. Dreams are a bridge between the conscious and the unconscious. Besides dreams, the unknown elements of the psyche extend themselves into the imagination that motivates literary works. The characters of the novel or story are "*representatives*" of the "*functional complexes in the psyche of the author*". In other words, particular psychic forces or emotions that are seeking entry into the conscious appear as psychological conflict points or "*complexes*" that each character embodies.

Jung's ideas are classified as "depth psychology" because he emphasizes the psychological necessity of "*turning away from outer things*" and exploring the inner things of the mind or psyche. This is what he did himself for a lifetime of inner exploration. This is what he taught his patients to do, and his approach is being carried forward under the contemporary practice of "analytical psychology". When Jung turned his focus inward he discovered the unconscious world or the world of the psyche. By this discovery he was able to forge into new territory for psychology, light years ahead of the slow moving behavioral and Freudian psychologists.

Freud used dream analysis in his psychiatric practice and theory, and wrote a book on dream analysis that became well known throughout society in Western countries. But there is no comparison between Freud's artificial and subjective approach to dream analysis, and that of Jung which is empirical, universal, and objective. Freud's dream analysis is personal, arbitrary, and unrelated to the actual psyche. Freud's idea of the unconscious was individual and personal, whereas Jung's idea of the unconscious is collective and universal. Freud's symbolism is ad hoc and commonsensical, while the symbolism used by Jung is not Jung's symbolism but nature's. It belongs to the human race. Freud invented his symbols; Jung discovered them.

Freud was a dedicated atheist. He did not mind writing publicly that people who believe in God are stuck in an immature childhood phase, needing the idea of an imaginary all powerful "father figure" to relate to. To believe in God was a psychological abnormality, according to Freud's atheistic bias.

But Jung on the other hand wrote that everything begins and ends with God. Jung revealed that throughout all his life God was at the center of all his ideas and motives. Jung always tried to get his patients back into their childhood religion or idea of God. He observed that those who listened to him got better, while others did not. Jung felt that all of modern society's psychopathology and unhappiness was caused by a wrong idea of and relationship with God.

By studying both religion and dreams Jung discovered "*the age-old fact that God speaks chiefly through dreams and visions*". This is also the theme in Swedenborg's works that show abundantly how the people, places, numbers, and objects mentioned in the Old and New Testaments are correspondences because God speaks only through parables, representatives, and correspondences.

Knowledge of psychology only comes with knowledge of the unconscious. ~Carl Jung, ETH, Alchemy, p. 224

Our consciousness originated in the unconscious. ~Carl Jung, ETH, Alchemy, p. 224

The fact is that if one tries beyond one's capacity to be perfect, the shadow descends into hell and becomes the devil. ~Carl Jung, Visions Seminar, p. 569

The more the libido is invested —or, to be more accurate, invests itself—in the unconscious, the greater becomes its influence or potency: all the rejected, disused, outlived functional possibilities that have been lost for generations come to life again and begin to exert an ever increasing influence on the conscious mind, despite its desperate struggles to gain insight into what is happening.

The saving factor is the symbol, which embraces both conscious and unconscious and unites them. For while the consciously disposable libido gets gradually used in the differentiated function and is replenished more and more slowly and with increasing difficulty, the symptoms of inner disunity multiply and there is a growing danger of inundation and destruction by the unconscious contents, but all the time the symbol is developing that is destined to resolve the conflict.

The symbol, however, is so intimately bound up with the dangerous and menacing aspect of the unconscious that it is easily mistaken for it, or its appearance may actually call forth evil and destructive tendencies. At all events the appearance of the redeeming symbol is closely connected with destruction and devastation.

If the old were not ripe for death, nothing new would appear; and if the old were not injuriously blocking the way for the new; it could not and need not be rooted out. ~Carl Jung, CW 6, Para 446

Individuation
Within Collectivity

As a psychotherapist I do not by any means try to deliver my patients from fear. Rather, I lead them to the reason for their fear, and then it becomes clear that it is justified. ~Carl Jung, Letters Vol. 1, p. 398

Jung argued that the psychological health of individuals and nations has been gradually degraded and is sick, both mentally and physically. I am reminded of Hobbes's saying that *homo homini lupus est* ("man to man is a wolf"). This leads to the perennial issue of why human beings are so deranged that they engage in conflict and savage hostility towards each other. We see this human savagery graphically exposed in the Bible, which is a historical and symbolic record of humanity being evil to humanity, and to God. Jung connects this negativity to the fact that "*our consciousness has strayed too far from its foundations and run into an impasse*".

One of the more striking images that Jung draws is that individuals are still "*undifferentiated from each other*" due to the "*participation mystique by which society contains the individual*". This seems to refer to an apparent opposition between collectivity and individuality. Society discourages individuality as a threat to itself. Jung says that the "*the mechanisms of convention keep people unconscious.*" But this is a false expectation and an illusory opposition. According to Jung's perception the individual in society is a "piece of the archetype". This unique individual piece has been "*differentiated out of the collective representation*".

Swedenborg's work shows that the more collective societies become, the more uniquely expressive are its members. Collectivity in its highest perfection is defined as a unity made up of unique individuals. The more advanced the individuation process of each person, the more perfectly can that person contribute to the collectivity.

Jung wrote:

> The participation mystique by which society contains the individual may be understood as a statement of the fact that individuals are still undifferentiated from each other, that is to say, they have not yet been self-consciously broken up into individual personalities. ~Carl Jung, C.G. Jung Speaking; Interviews and Encounters, p. 205-218

> The archetype of the individual is the Self. The Self is all embracing. God is a circle whose center is everywhere and whose circumference is

nowhere. ~Carl Jung, C.G. Jung Speaking; Interviews and Encounters, p. 205-218

The individual in society may be understood as a piece of the archetype, a piece that has been differentiated out of the collective representation. ~Carl Jung, C.G. Jung Speaking; Interviews and Encounters, p. 205-218

The mechanisms of convention . . . keep people unconscious. ~Carl Jung, C.G. Jung Speaking; Interviews and Encounters, p. 205-218

Human beings are created to grow by stages. Jung has diagnosed and has pointed to the consequences of resisting the process of growth and wanting to remain at one stage of development. Jung wants us to analyze our dreams and inspect them in the light of major historical events and mythical characters. This will allow us to return to our humanity by progressing with our spiritual growth towards *"our basic human nature"*.

Looking at our dreams in the light of mythology brings us the deep insight and experience that our dreams are collective and have a collective meaning. This feeling validates our humanity and consequent relationship to God whom Swedenborg calls the "original Human" and the "only Human in itself". All humanity in human beings originates from this original and infinite Human of God. Swedenborg frequently uses the expression the "Divine Human" when referring to God.

Jung has elevated the ordinary dreaming that we all do to a new level of spiritual reality. No one dreams alone and merely subjectively, as Freud believed. Jung tells us that our dreams are objective natural phenomena consisting of events of a collective nature, just like history and literature, some of which is local and some universal. This deep idea greatly enhances the experience of self and being a human being. The essence of being human is our collectivity. Individuation is the attainment of genuine collectivity. This seems like a paradox so I'll explain further.

The apparent contradiction is resolved when we consider that individuation and collectivity are not opposites but reciprocals. The perfect and healthy collectivity is an aggregate composed of healthy individuals. There is no collectivity other than the collection of individuals. Nor is it the case that the individuals in a collectivity are uniform and non-varying or non-expressive of individuality. In fact the opposite is the case. One is more and more unique as an individual when being part of a unified collection of other unique individuals.

Swedenborg explained that the perfection of a collectivity increases in proportion to (a) the uniqueness of each component or individual; and (b) the total number of individuals in the collectivity. If two individuals were uniform or less contrastive, then the perfection of the collectivity would be reduced. Also, if the size of the collectivity were to be reduced, then its perfection also would diminish.

Swedenborg explained that the numberless heavenly zones in the human mind constantly keep increasing in size and variety of unique individuals present. These arrive every day and hour from all the inhabited planets of the natural universe, increasing the size of both the heavens and the hells in the human mind. Every person is involved in this process since everyone's mind is in the same mental world. *Hence if heavens and hells multiply they do so in every human being's mind.*

Jung saw individuation as a process of becoming more and more the individual we were born to be and grow into. This is part of being a human being. It takes growth to become mature and healthy. Modern civilization, with its focus on materialism and its hostility towards spirituality, has arrested individuation and normal human growth. The unconscious mythology of archetypes are psychic nourishment for this mental and emotional growth process. We become less human if we oppose our unconscious. We become primitive, savage, inhuman. Homo homini lupus est.

The causal factors determining his psychic existence reside largely in unconscious processes outside consciousness, and in the same way there are final factors at work in him which likewise originate in the unconscious. ~Carl Jung, Aion, Para 253

Sexuality: Freud, Jung, and Swedenborg

I will describe to you what I have learned from the work of Jung and Swedenborg. I tried to estimate how much each has written or published by collecting all their books and writings in one big computer file. I believe that I got about 90 percent of their total output. The word processor then gave me the totals for how many times a particular word appeared. I added Freud, as I was also interested in his work in relation to Jung. I published the analysis in the *Journal of Psychology and Clinical Psychiatry* in 2015.

In order to give you an opportunity to explore the numbers, I reproduce the main table below so that you can see a contrast between these three giants of psychology. I also include my explanations from an earlier draft of the published article.

Table 1a shows the conceptual focus of the three writers measured by the number of occurrences of selected words in the Collected Works of Freud, Jung, and Swedenborg:

Table 1a Keywords for Freud, Jung, and Swedenborg			
	Freud *Complete Works* (1856– 1939)	**Jung** *Collected Works* (1875 - 1961)	**Swedenborg** *Complete Writings* (1688- 1772)
Number of words and pages in print	2 million 2,500	3 million 3,000	5 million 7,000
Frequency of Occurrence of Certain Words			
Archetype	0	1,982	1
Body	592	2,112	1,888
Charity	5	16	1,734

Child(ren)	**4,441**	**3,347**	780
God etc. *(**1)*	1,437	**8,032**	**18,394**
Conscience	215	281	906
Conscious(ness)	**2,314**	**16,538**	282
Devil, demon, satan, genii, evil spirits	552	1,697	1,324
Ego, self	**2,982**	**9,954**	**4,426**
Energy	350	1,075	61
Father	**2,474**	1,908	**4,824**
Heaven	80	1,181	**4,832**
Hell	54	413	**2,723**
Immortal(ity)	56	337	44
Incest	190	483	362
Instinct	**3,203**	2,020	188
Love	**2,062**	1,890	**4,581**
Mind, mental	**4,189**	**5,345**	**2,261**
Mother	1,701	**3,284**	1,367
Myth	273	2,035	36
Proprium	0	2	745
Psyche, psychical	**2,039**	**3,268**	3
Religion	574	1,240	1,334
Sacred	108	284	1,149
Sex topics *(**2)*	**3,557**	**4,268**	**11,761**
Soul	184	1,055	1,254
Spirits/spiritual	345	**4,763**	**3,598**
Swedenborg	1	40	0
Symbol	791	**6,244**	707
Synchronicity	0	283	0
Taboo	556	127	2
The Word, Sacred Scripture, Bible	38	683	**6,083**
Unconscious	**2,373**	**9,002**	51

Table 1a Footnotes (see in Table)

1. **Includes: *God, Christ, Jesus, Lord, Divine, Jehovah, Yahweh*
2. **Sex topics: the following words all but the last appear in Freud; some also occur in Jung and in Swedenborg:

Erotic/sexuality/sex/vagina/penis/sexual
intercourse/orgasm/coitus/clitoris/scortatory/deflowering/virgin/hymen
/masturbation/whore/seduction/ prostitute/ harlot/genitals

Table 1b Their Intense Topic Focus Measured by Most Frequently Occurring Words			
	Freud	**Jung**	**Swedenborg**
Child(ren)	**4,441**	**3,347**	780
God	1,437	**8,032**	**18,394**
Conscious(ness)	**2,314**	**16,538**	282
Ego, self	**2,982**	**9,954**	**4,426**
Father	**2,474**	1,908	**4,824**
Heaven	80	1,181	**4,832**
Hell	54	413	**2,723**
Love	**2,062**	1,890	**4,581**
Mind, mental	**4,189**	**5,345**	**2,261**
Mother	1,701	**3,284**	1,367
Psyche, psychical	**2,039**	**3,268**	3
Sex topics *(1)*	**3,557**	**4,268**	**11,761**
Spirits/spiritual	345	**4,763**	**3,598**
Symbol	791	**6,244**	707
Sacred Scripture /the Word/ Bible	38	683	**6,083**
Unconscious	**2,373**	**9,002**	51

One should keep in mind that these comparisons are relative and based on imprecise data and should be viewed as suggestive only.

By looking at Table 1b we can get a comparison of what topics the three authors held in their focus. First, by looking up and down within a column you can see the most frequent number of occurrences bolded for each author. Second, by looking across the rows you can compare the overlap between them.

Freud kept his most intense focus on the topics of *Child, Conscious, Ego/self, Father, Love, Mind/mental, Psyche, Unconscious, and Sex topics.*

Jung kept his most intense focus on the topics of *Child, God, Conscious, Ego/self, Mind/mental, Mother, Psyche, Spirits/spiritual, Unconscious, Symbol, and Sex topics.*

Swedenborg kept his most intense focus on the topics of *God, Self, Father, Heaven and Hell, Love, Mind/mental, Spirits/spiritual, Sacred Scripture, and Sex topics.*

The two-way overlap between Freud and Jung includes a focus on *Child, Consciousness, Ego/Self, Mind/mental, Psyche, Unconscious, and Sex topics.*

The two-way overlap between Freud and Swedenborg includes a focus on *Ego/self, Father, Love, Mind/mental, and Sex topics.*

The two-way overlap between Jung and Swedenborg includes a focus on *God, Ego/self, Mind/mental, Spirits/spiritual, and Sex topics.*

The three-way overlap between Freud, Jung, and Swedenborg includes a focus on *Ego/self, Mind/mental, and Sex topics.*

It is significant that all three writers maintain an intense focus on sex topics but in quite different ways. As will be seen later in this book Swedenborg frequently discussed the *spiritual* sense of such frequently mentioned words in the Bible as whore, harlot, adultery, whoredom, lusting, and fornication. These references in *Sacred Scripture* to unlawful sexual activity always refer to *mental* fornication and *spiritual* whoredom, indicating by correspondence to the falsification of the truths given in *Sacred Scripture*. Such frequent mention and dire warnings occur in the *Old Testament* respecting falsification of spiritual truths is because the truths of *Sacred Scripture* are the only means people have for their regeneration and consequent salvation.

People falsify truths in their own mind in order to justify and keep on hating the neighbor and lusting after the neighbor's honors, spouse, and possessions. Once these truths are falsified in an individual's mind there is no avenue left for regeneration and salvation. The consequence for the person is called "death" which refers to "spiritual death", which is a life in hell. Hence is the great importance of this topic for Swedenborg.

Freud's focus on sex topics was strictly natural, psychological, and biological. He did not himself discuss spiritual topics because he was an atheist. But he often refers to the religion and "superstitious" beliefs of his patients. Sexuality for Freud was involved in biology and the individual unconscious psyche, where repressed ideas resided, sometimes threatening to spring out into the open, an event which his patients greatly feared on account of the emotions and desires these taboo ideas would reveal about the person. One of the best known ideas in this respect is Freud's description of the "Oedipus complex" in infantile and childhood sexuality.

Jung's focus on sex-topics was their mythical significance and their appearance in the patient's conscious as erotic fantasies. Jung acknowledged the significance of sexuality in human life. After examining the results he obtained from his word association tests given to patients, Jung concluded: "*Finally, it may be permissible to point out once more that an overwhelming number of the complexes we have discovered in our subjects are erotic. In view of the great part played by love and sexuality in human life, this is not surprising*" (Jung, *Studies In Word Association: The Associations Of Normal Subjects*, p. 381)

Well, there you have it. I know it may not clear what these kinds of data tell us about the authors. It fits in with one of my research areas called *psycholinguistics*. A general principle is that one can estimate what a community or group is talking about by counting what are the most frequently used words people say or write. The web search engine giant

Goggle that everyone knows, regularly posts what the most searched words were on a particular day, or after something happened that captured the national news. So you are probably familiar with that idea, and it has face validity or meaning.

I want to comment on the finding that all three psychologists maintained an intense focus on what I called "sex-topics". I specify in footnote 2 of Table 1a above what are the various sex-related words that I lumped together. I also point out the important fact that Freud's references to sexuality were purely physical and biological as applied to the mind when it is defined as the activity of the physical brain. This is still the single view of modern psychology and neuroscience. In contrast to this, Jung and Swedenborg were more interested in the spiritual meaning to which these sexuality words corresponded or what they symbolized about the universal human experience.

More than half of Swedenborg's writings consist of a word-by-word analysis of the Old and New Testaments in the Bible. Swedenborg's discussions on sex topics were for the most part explanations of the sex topics that appear so frequently in the Bible, especially in the Prophets of the *Old Testament*. Swedenborg's work shows that the spiritual meaning of every sex related word in the Bible, such as *fornication*, *adultery*, *whoredom*, *harlot*, and *lusting after the neighbor's wife*, refer to *mental* fornication and *spiritual* whoredom. These signify by correspondence the falsification of spiritual truths given in *Sacred Scripture*.

These truths are necessary for the regeneration of every individual since without them no one can be successful in fighting the spiritual battles in regeneration. Hence it is that God discusses these topics frequently as a way of warning us that we must not falsify spiritual truths or precipitate ourselves into the punishment of hell that resides in self-love and selfishness. *Sacred Scripture* provides these spiritual truths in the form of religious commandments, and when the people "adulterate" these truths to justify selfish reasons and unlawful acts, they become falsified truths that cannot defeat our temptations. As a result we remain in our selfish personality, and this eventually devolves into a life of hell in eternity. Hence is the importance of this topic for Swedenborg.

Jung also regards sexuality and love as psychic forces that are biological, but not merely physical, as it is in Freud's psychology. Jung defines wholeness of the individual as a sexual union or integration between the masculine *animus* portions and the feminine *anima* portion that constitute every ego-personality. Without this integration within the individual the process of individuation cannot proceed, leaving the person as a collective general without a unique individual identity and potential.

In Swedenborg the affective portion of the mind is feminine while the cognitive portion is masculine. He asserts that nothing is more important in psychology than to understand how these two systems form a union that he calls the *spiritual marriage*. This meaning is derived from the *Divine marriage*, which is the union of the Father-function and the Son-function in God, thus of affective love with cognitive intelligence. Moreover, both Jung and Swedenborg discuss the union formed by a man and a woman in marriage love as the center of psychic development. Only in this mental union between husband and wife can the wholeness of each individual achieve perfection and full potential. It is in this *conjugial unity*, whereby two minds become one mind, that the creation of a human being can reach its perfection in eternity.

Dreams and Psychic Health

Dreams are impartial, spontaneous products of the unconscious psyche, outside the control of the will. They are pure nature; they show us the unvarnished, natural truth, and are therefore fitted, as nothing else is, to give us back an attitude that accords with our basic human nature when our consciousness has strayed too far from its foundations and run into an impasse. ~Carl Jung, The Meaning of Psychology for Modern Man, 1933. In CW 10: Civilization in Transition, p. 317

If, in addition to this, we bear in mind that the unconscious contains everything that is lacking to consciousness, that the unconscious therefore has a compensatory tendency, then we can begin to draw conclusions-provided, of course, that the dream does not come from too deep a psychic level. If it is a dream of this kind, it will as a rule contains mythological motifs, combinations of ideas or images which can be found in the myths of one's own folk or in those of other races. The dream will then have a collective meaning, a meaning which is the common property of mankind. ~Carl Jung, The Meaning of Psychology for Modern Man, 1933. In CW 10: Civilization in Transition, pg. 322.

One would do well to treat every dream as though it were a totally unknown object. Look at it from all sides, take it in your hand, carry it about with you, let your imagination play round it, and talk about it with other people. ~Carl Jung, The Meaning of Psychology for Modern Man, 1933. In CW 10: Civilization in Transition, p. 320

Dreams are not under our conscious control. They are "*spontaneous products of the unconscious psyche*". Dreams are produced by raw nature in the human mind and therefore puts us back into alignment with nature such as human beings exist. Dreams restore us to the reality of what we are, namely psychic beings of the unconscious. This is the foundation of human nature from which society has departed, turning instead to artificial meanings and images that have no underlying psychological reality.

Dreams restore us to psychic health and deliver us from the "impasse" of civilized life or non-life known as the "*collective mentality*", which is a psychopathological state in which the individual becomes "*estranged from himself*" and living in "*conventional morality*".

A dream that is not understood remains a mere occurrence; understood it becomes a living experience. ~Carl Jung CW11; p. 497

Religion vs. Creed

Jung makes a distinction between genuine religion and a creed. While religion remains true to the process of individuation, a creed is the politicization of religion causing its spiritual death in the mind of the members. A creed is a falsified and dead religion. A genuine and living religion fosters a personal relationship with God that promotes responsibility, mental health, and continuous individuation through that relationship.

> *Religion, however, teaches another authority opposed to that of the "world." The doctrine of the individual's dependence on God makes just as high a claim upon him as the world does. It may even happen that the absoluteness of this claim estranges him from the world in the same way as he is estranged from himself when he succumbs to the collective mentality. He can forfeit his judgment and power of decision in the former case (for the sake of religious doctrine) quite as much as in the latter.*

> *This is the goal which religion openly aspires to unless it compromises with the State. When it does so, I prefer to call it not "religion" but a "creed." A creed gives expression to a definite collective belief, whereas the word religion expresses a subjective relationship to certain metaphysical, extramundane factors. A creed is a confession of faith intended chiefly for the world at large and is thus an intramundane affair, while the meaning and purpose of religion lie in the relationship of the individual to God (Christianity, Judaism, Islam) or to the path of salvation and liberation (Buddhism).*

> *From this basic fact all ethics is derived, which without the individual's responsibility before God can be called nothing more than conventional morality. ~Carl Jung, The Undiscovered Self*

> *Consequently, the work of salvation is intended to save man from the fear of God. ~Carl Jung, CW 11, Para 659*

What is ordinarily called "religion" is a substitute to such an amazing degree that I ask myself seriously whether this kind of "religion," which I prefer to call a creed, may not after all have an important function in human society. ~Carl Jung, CW 11, Para 75

In my profession I have encountered many people who have had immediate experience and who would not and could not submit to the authority of ecclesiastical decision. ~Carl Jung, CW 11, Para 76

Dreams Possess
Collective Meaning

Another striking image that Jung gives us is that dreams are the "*common property*" to humankind.

Dreams possess "*collective meaning*". The evidence for this is that people's dreams contain "*mythological motifs, combinations of ideas or images which can be found in the myths of one's own folk or in those of other races*". Much of Jung's psychology is centered on the notion of the "archetypes" that exist in the collective unconscious of humankind. Archetypes emerge from the depths of the psyche of individual human beings around the world independently of culture or religion. All religions incorporate symbols, symbolisms, correspondences, and representatives that connect to particular psychological functions built anatomically into the human mind.

Both Jung and Swedenborg made extensive studies of symbolism. Jung focused on dream manifestations and cross-cultural religious symbols. Swedenborg focused on the spiritual symbolism in the Old and New Testaments. He called these symbols "*correspondences*" and demonstrates how correspondences are used to extract the spiritual meaning from the verses and phrases of Sacred Scripture.

For both Jung and Swedenborg the human mind is an anatomical structure that has substance, organic structure, form and shape, but no material elements, spaces, or times. Hence it is that the unconscious world is a substantive world that contains psychic objects, forces, and qualities.

In Jung's language we are born with a conscious mind that defines our ego and changes over time as it develops and evolves through recurrent experiences. This conscious growing ego-personality is anatomically connected to the collective unconscious, which is the larger collective entity that is shared with every human individual from birth onwards.

An individual human mind is therefore an anatomical structure connected to all other human beings through the shared collective unconscious. "*Psychology*" refers to the personal management strategies by which an individual mind administers itself. This involves guarding the doorway between the individual conscious mind and the shared collective unconscious.

Jung studied the details of this management technique by analyzing the thoughts and dreams of his patients as well as his own. He reported the details of how people are prone to keep the gate of unconsciousness tightly shut in the face of important personal information from the unconscious. Personality structure refers to the character of the psychological complexes with which the person gets stuck. Unresolved complexes accumulate from birth onward. They are strategies by which the ego gatekeeper keeps the critical information out of conscious awareness. This self-destructive style of living produces a variety of psychological complexes that lead to de-individuation and an inauthentic life.

In this impoverished and reduced state of human living the individual has no control over emotions and is constantly being attacked by unconscious psychic forces that should have been admitted and examined, but instead were kept out. By keeping this critical knowledge from becoming part of the ego, human beings have set each other up to be immersed in persistent conflicts with the environment, the ego, and each other, that show themselves in the form of destruction of the environment, neurotic personalities, broken relationships, falsified relationship with God, criminality and injustice, and internecine wars.

> *As the individual is not just a single, separate being, but by his very existence presupposes a collective relationship, it follows that the process of individuation must lead to more intense and broader collective relationships and not to isolation.*
> ~Carl Jung, Definitions, CW 6, par. 758

Jung realized that if the psychic world is a real world then it must be made of something rather than nothing, and the objects that exist in that world must be real organic forms that have an anatomy, structure, and shape. If archetypes are to be considered real they must have some substance, form, and organic anatomy. Without this there is no objective reality or empirical permanence to something.

Jung asserted that dreams create these "psychic forms" through meaningful themes or "motifs" such as the variety of universal archetypes that people report in their dreams. These psychic forms are organic objects that have permanent existence in the collective unconscious. They existed before any individual dreamer was born. In the analysis of dreams one can ascertain the presence of such archetypal motifs.

Jung talked about two types of dreams. "*Little dreams*" are involvements with the everyday affairs. They are personal, subjective, and adventitious. They are quickly forgotten due to their lack of deeper significance. "*Significant dreams*" are rich in psychic content and tend to be remembered a long time.

The richness of psychic content comes from the collective property of the unconscious. Jung said that dreams contain "*everything that has ever been of significance in the life of humanity*". Jung believed that all of the human sciences need to be unified and brought to bear on dream analysis in order to have sufficient "interpretive equipment" to fit the puzzle pieces together that give coherence to the cumulative totality of human experience.

> *The human begins in the inmost of the rational, and extends itself thence to man's external.* ~Swedenborg, Arcana Coelestia, AC 2106

> *Only those who touch bottom can rally be human."* ~Carl Jung, Visions Seminar, p. 394

All of Jung's analytical and depth psychology is encapsulated in this one quote above, namely that we begin to be human only when we explore and discover what lies in our mind, which Jung calls "touching bottom". As the parallel Swedenborg quote indicates, that beginning of becoming human is the rational mind. The depth of the human mind involves its layers of mental anatomy which functions more perfectly as our knowledge and consciousness are removed from the external personality and moved inward into its depth.

The anatomical layer of the "external" mind functions to provide us with our consciousness, knowledge, and understanding that are applied to the natural world and environment. This is the external layer of our mind that is formed in childhood through sensory input and experience. The ideas and concepts operating at this sensory-motor level are sense-bound, time-bound, matter-bound, and measurement-bound. This level of thinking is called "materialism" in philosophy and science. In Swedenborg it is called "*natural consciousness*" and is a level of psychic functioning that is adapted to the conditions of our physical environment. But when our consciousness goes inward a layer, we immediately begin to function with ideas and concepts that are applied to the spiritual or mental world. This is called spiritual consciousness.

The human mind is anatomically structured in layers of differential functioning. The outmost layer is natural consciousness as just mentioned, which has three sub-layers. The second layer as we dig down is spiritual consciousness or functioning and it too has three sub-layers. The first layer of spiritual consciousness functions with ideas and reasoning that recognize the details of natural consciousness as being merely appearances that symbolize or represent the events in the deeper spiritual layer of consciousness. Natural consciousness may be equated with what Jung called ego-consciousness. Spiritual consciousness is in the plane of the collective unconscious.

Self-analysis and healthy development involve raising consciousness from natural to spiritual, or in Jung's terms, allowing elements of the unconscious to cross the gap and enter consciousness. When this occurs, functioning in spiritual consciousness is achieved and the person becomes more truly individuated and uniquely differentiated from the others in the collective.

Note that spiritual functioning occurs in a distinct anatomical layer that is located within the depth of the natural mind and consciousness. When the unconscious spiritual functioning that operates within surfaces into the awareness of natural consciousness, it provides the awareness of spiritual consciousness and functioning in our natural awareness. This joint and synchronous operation between the two layers of the mind greatly enhances and enriches the perfection or quality of functioning of a human being. It is really only at this level of the spiritual within the natural that marks the beginning of being human. Below that we function like merely higher animals, having language and symbolic communication that allow them to operate with higher cognitions and symbols.

Yet these "human-animal" cognitions are not genuinely human but pre-human, with the potential of becoming human if these are enriched by spiritual cognitions.

The Art of
Interpreting Dreams

This is the secret of dreams—that we do not dream, but rather we are dreamt. ~Carl Jung, Children's Dreams Seminar, P 159

So difficult is it to understand a dream that for a long time I have made it a rule, when someone tells me a dream and asks for my
opinion, to say first of all to myself: "I have no idea what this dream means." ~Carl Jung, CW 8, Para 533

If we want to interpret a dream correctly, we need a thorough knowledge of the conscious situation at that moment, because the dream contains its unconscious complement, that is, the material which the conscious situation has constellated in the unconscious. Without this knowledge it is impossible to interpret a dream correctly, except by a lucky fluke. ~Carl Jung, CW 8, Para 477

For there are certain happenings in the development of the human psyche where things become particularly confused and dark, and people become incoherent and cannot express themselves.

Situations come up in dreams which seemed to be very clear, but as soon as you are back in the conscious state, everything is blurred and you find it exceedingly difficult to describe what you actually experienced; you have no words to explain those intricate situations.

There are many thoughts which cannot be thought clearly; and there are many inner experiences which are apparent only to the inner eye or heart-whatever you like to call that organ. It seems perfectly simple there, but human language is inadequate, and then people take to drawing.

Also, certain experiences in dreams or visions are so expressive, so full of color and plastic life that they recommend themselves to the dreamer, and he naturally yields to the temptation to reproduce what he has seen.

So there are all sorts of reasons why people take to it. Of course, when I see that the quality of my patients' experiences suggests representation, I encourage them, because I have learned through long experience-about fourteen years when to encourage the people to whom it is useful. It helps them to concretize inner events.

For most people are suffering from the prejudice that they are not real because they cannot be handled, or even talked about in a logical way. In such a case the drawing is invaluable. It concretizes; it makes a statement so that other people can see it. It is there in reality as if painted on the wall; they begin to think that it does exist. ~Carl Jung, Visions Seminar, Page 4

In the Old Testament [Genesis 41] we read about Joseph in Egypt who made a reputation for himself as an interpreter of dreams. When Pharaoh had a disturbing dream he sought the help of his court magicians and wise men, but they could not give the king a satisfactory answer. Pharaoh was then told about Joseph and summoned him to the court. When Joseph arrived and was told the details of the dream, he gave an interpretation that Pharaoh could accept and act upon.

Genesis 41. And it happened at the end of two years of days, that Pharaoh was dreaming, and behold, he was standing next to the river. And behold, out of the river seven cows were coming up, beautiful in appearance and fat-fleshed; and they fed in the sedge. And behold, seven other cows were coming up after them out of the river, bad in appearance and thin-fleshed, and stood by the [other] cows on the bank of the river. And the cows bad in appearance and thin-fleshed devoured the seven cows beautiful in appearance and fat. And Pharaoh awoke. ... And Pharaoh sent and called Joseph. ... And Joseph said to Pharaoh, Pharaoh's dream, it is one; what God is doing He has pointed out to Pharaoh.

The seven good cows are seven years, and the seven good heads of grain are seven years; the dream, it is one. And the seven thin and bad cows coming up after them are seven years; and the seven empty heads of grain, scorched by an east wind, will be seven years of famine.

Behold, seven years are coming, [in which there will be] a great abundance of corn in all the land of Egypt. And seven years of famine will arise after them, and all the abundance of corn in the land of Egypt will be thrust into oblivion, and the famine will consume the land. And the abundance of corn in the land will not be known because of the famine from then on, for it will be extremely severe. ...

Swedenborg discusses this passage and gives its spiritual meaning that was extracted by means of correspondences. The analysis is very involved but can be summarized by this: "*In the internal sense of this chapter the subject treated of is the second state of the celestial of the spiritual, which is "Joseph," in its elevation above what is of the natural or external man, and so above all the memory-knowledges therein, which are "Egypt."*" (AC 5191) In other words, the spiritual content concerns details about the ordered steps of mental growth and development during regeneration. But Swedenborg also gives us explanations about the literal sense, which concerns dreams.

As regards dreams, it is known that the Lord revealed the arcana of heaven to the prophets, not only by visions, but also by dreams, and that the dreams were as fully representative and significative as the visions, being almost of the same class; and that to others also as well as the prophets things to come were disclosed by dreams; as by the dreams of Joseph, and of those who were in prison with him, and by those of Pharaoh, of Nebuchadnezzar, and others, from which it may be seen that dreams of this kind, equally with visions, flow in from heaven; with this difference, that dreams occur when the corporeal is asleep, and visions when it is not asleep. How prophetic dreams, and such as are found in the Word, flow in, nay, descend from heaven, has been shown me to the life; concerning which I may relate the following particulars, from experience. ~Swedenborg, Arcana Coelestia 1975

There are three kinds of dreams. The first kind come from the Lord mediately through heaven; such were the prophetic dreams that are treated of in the Word. The second kind come through angelic spirits, especially those who are in front above at the right, where there are paradisal scenes; from this source the men of the Most Ancient Church had their dreams, which were instructive (see n. 1122). The third kind come through the spirits who are near when man is sleeping, which are likewise significative. But fantastic dreams come from a different source. ~Swedenborg, Arcana Coelestia 1976

More information from Swedenborg on dreams is presented in the next chapter.

Now, continuing with Jung on dreams:

To concern ourselves with dreams is a way of reflecting on ourselves-a way of self-reflection. It is not our ego-consciousness reflecting on itself; rather, it turns its attention to the objective actuality of the dream as a communication or message from the unconscious, unitary soul of humanity. It reflects not on the ego but on the self; it recollects that strange self, alien to the ego, which was ours from the beginning, the trunk from which the ego grew. It is alien to us because we have estranged ourselves from it through the aberrations of the conscious mind. ~Carl Jung, The Meaning of Psychology for Modern Man, 1933. In CW 10: Civilization in Transition, pg. 318.

The dream is often occupied with apparently very silly details, thus producing an impression of absurdity, or else it is on the surface so unintelligible as to leave us thoroughly bewildered. Hence we always have to overcome a certain resistance before we can seriously set about disentangling the intricate web through patient work. But when at last we penetrate to its real meaning, we find ourselves deep in the dreamer's secrets and discover with astonishment that an apparently quite senseless dream is in the highest degree significant, and that in reality it speaks only of important and serious matters. ~Carl Jung, On the Psychology of the Unconscious, 1953

In sleep, fantasy takes the form of dreams. But in waking life, too, we continue to dream beneath the threshold of consciousness, especially when under the influence of repressed or other unconscious complexes. ~Carl Jung, Problems of Modern Self-analysis, 1929. In CW 16: The Practice of Self-analysis. p. 125

One would do well to treat every dream as though it were a totally unknown object. Look at it from all sides, take it in your hand, carry it about with you, let your imagination play round it, and talk about it with other people. Primitives tell each other impressive dreams, in a public palaver if possible, and this custom is also attested in late antiquity, for all the ancient peoples attributed great significance to dreams '

Treated in this way, the dream suggests all manner of ideas and associations which lead us closer to its meaning. The ascertainment of the meaning is, I need hardly point out, an entirely arbitrary affair, and this is where the hazards begin. Narrower or wider limits will be set to the meaning, according to one's experience, temperament, and taste. Some people will be satisfied with little, for others much is still not enough.

Also the meaning of the dream, or our interpretation of it, is largely dependent on the intentions of the interpreter, on what he expects the meaning to be or requires it to do. In eliciting the meaning he will involuntarily be guided by certain presuppositions, and it depends very much on the scrupulousness and honesty of the investigator whether he gains something by his interpretation or perhaps only becomes still more deeply entangled in his mistakes. ~Carl Jung, The Meaning of Psychology for Modern Man, 1933. In CW 10: Civilization in Transition, p. 320

The art of interpreting dreams cannot be learnt from books. Methods and rules are good only when we can get along without them. Only the man who can do it anyway has real skill, only the man of understanding really understands. ~"The Meaning of Psychology for Modern Man" (1933). In CW 10: Civilization in Transition. P. 327

The dream is a little hidden door in the innermost and most secret recesses of the soul, opening into that cosmic night which was psyche long before there was any ego consciousness, and which will remain psyche no matter how far our ego-consciousness extends. For all ego-consciousness is isolated; because it separates and discriminates, it knows only particulars, and it sees only those that can be related to the ego. Its essence is limitation, even though it reaches to the farthest nebulae among the stars. All consciousness separates; but in dreams we put on the likeness of that more universal, truer, more eternal man dwelling in the darkness of primordial night. There he is still the whole, and the whole is in him, indistinguishable from nature and bare of all egohood. It is from these all-uniting depths that the dream arises, be it never so childish, grotesque, and immoral. ~Carl Jung, The Meaning of Psychology for Modern Man, 1933. In CW 10: Civilization in Transition, p. 304

When we consider the infinite variety of dreams, it is difficult to conceive that there could ever be a method or a technical procedure which would lead to an infallible result. It is, indeed, a good thing that no valid method exists, for otherwise the meaning of the dream would be limited in advance and would lose precisely that virtue which makes dreams so valuable for therapeutic purposes -their ability to offer new points of view. ~Carl Jung, The Meaning of Psychology for Modern Man, 1933. In CW 10: Civilization in Transition, p. 319

Lack of conscious understanding does not mean that the dream has no effect at all. Even civilized man can occasionally observe that a dream which he cannot remember can slightly alter his mood for better or worse. Dreams can be "understood" to a certain extent in a subliminal way, and that is mostly how they work. ~Carl Jung, Approaching the Unconscious In Man and His Symbols

The dream is often occupied with apparently very silly details, thus producing an impression of absurdity, or else it is on the surface so unintelligible as to leave us thoroughly bewildered. Hence we always have to overcome a certain resistance before we can seriously set about disentangling the intricate web through patient work. But when at last we penetrate to its real meaning, we find ourselves deep in the dreamer's secrets and discover with astonishment that an apparently quite senseless dream is in the highest degree significant, and that in reality it speaks only of important and serious matters. This discovery compels rather more respect for the so-called superstition that dreams have a meaning, to which the rationalistic temper of our age has hitherto given short shrift. ~"On the Psychology of the Unconscious" (1953). In CW 7: Two Essays on Analytical Psychology. P. 24

The conscious mind allows itself to be trained like a parrot, but the unconscious does not — which is why St. Augustine thanked God for not making him responsible for his dreams. ~Psychology and Alchemy p. 51

As individuals we are not completely unique, but are like all other men. Hence a dream with a collective meaning is valid in the first place for the dreamer, but it expresses at the same time the fact that his momentary problem is also the problem of other people. This is often of great practical importance, for there are countless people who are inwardly cut off from humanity and oppressed by the thought that nobody else has their problems.

Or else they are those all-too modest souls who, feeling themselves nonentities, have kept their claim to social recognition on too low a level. Moreover, every individual problem is somehow connected with the problem of the age, so that practically every subjective difficulty has to be viewed from the standpoint of the human situation as a whole. But this is permissible only when the dream really is a mythological one and makes use of collective symbols. ~Carl Jung, CW 10, Para 323

We must now turn to the question of how the existence of archetypes can be proved. Since archetypes are supposed to produce certain psychic forms, we must discuss how and where one can get hold of the material demonstrating these forms. The main source, then, is dreams, which have the advantage of being involuntary, spontaneous products of nature not falsified by any conscious purpose. By questioning the individual one can ascertain which of the motifs appearing in the dream are known to him... Consequently, we must look for motifs which could not possibly be known to the dreamer and yet behave functionally of the archetype known from historical sources. ~Carl Jung, The Archetypes and the Collective Unconscious p. 48

Not all dreams are of equal importance. Even primitives distinguish between "little" and "big" dreams. ... "Little" dreams are the nightly fragments of fantasy coming from the subjective and personal sphere, and their meaning is limited to the affairs of everyday. That is why such dreams are easily forgotten, just because their validity extends no further than the day-to-day fluctuations of the psychic balance. Significant dreams, on the other hand, are often remembered for a lifetime, and not infrequently prove to be the richest jewel in the treasure house of psychic experience. ~Carl Jung, The Structure and Dynamics of the Psyche, 1960

A dream, like every element in the psychic structure, is a product of the total psyche. Hence we may expect to find in dreams everything that has ever been of significance in the life of humanity, just as human life is not limited to this or that fundamental instinct, but builds itself up from a multiplicity of instincts, needs, desires, and physical and psychic conditions, etc., so the dream cannot be explained by this or that element in it, however beguilingly simple such an explanation may appear to be. We can be certain that it is incorrect because no simple theory of instinct will ever be capable of grasping the human psyche, that mighty and mysterious thing, nor, consequently, its exponent, the dream. In order to do anything like justice to dreams, we need interpretive equipment that must be laboriously fitted together from all branches of the humane sciences. ~Carl Jung, General Aspects of Dream Psychology, 1916. In CW 8: The Structure and Dynamics of the Psyche, p. 527

Anyone sufficiently interested in the dream problem cannot have failed to observe that dreams also have continuity forwards-if such an expression be permitted-since dreams occasionally exert a remarkable influence on the conscious mental life even of persons who cannot be considered superstitious or particularly abnormal. ~Carl Jung, General Aspects of Dream Psychology, 1916. In CW 8: The Structure and Dynamics of the Psyche, p. 444

We Do Not Produce Dreams: They Come To Us

The "dream-ego" is the part of our personality that is conscious of the dream. We are not unconscious when dreaming. We are asleep which means that the cerebrum is not sufficiently active to be aware of external or physical sensory input. But the cerebellum is active and awake. The dream-ego is the witness to the incoming dreams. When we awake from sleep the cerebrum is active again. Now we can try to consciously "remember" the dream, which is possible because we have access to the dream-ego's memory of the events. Jung wrote:

> *As in our waking state, real people and things enter our field of vision, so the dream-images enter like another kind of reality into the field of consciousness of the dream-ego. We do not feel as if we were producing the dreams, it is rather as if the dreams came to us. They are not subject to our control but obey their own laws. They are obviously autonomous psychic complexes which form themselves out of their own material. We do not know the source of their motives, and we therefore say that dreams come from the unconscious. In saying this, we assume that there are independent psychic complexes which elude our conscious control and come and go according to their own laws. ~Carl Jung, The Psychological Foundations of Belief in Spirits, 1920. In CW 8: The Structure and Dynamics of the Psyche, p. 580*

As regards the much discussed symbolism of dreams, its evaluation varies according to whether it is considered from the causal or from the final standpoint. The causal approach of Freud starts from a desire or craving, that is, from the repressed dream-wish. This craving is always something comparatively simple and elementary, which can hide itself under manifold disguises.... Hence it is that the more rigorous adherents of the Freudian school have come to the point of interpreting-to give a gross example-pretty well all oblong objects in dreams as phallic symbols and all round or hollow objects as feminine symbols. ~Carl Jung, General Aspects of Dream Psychology (1916). In CW 8: The Structure and Dynamics of the Psyche, p. 470

There are two ways of conceptualizing the symbolic nature of dream events. One is to see the cause of the dream as some love that comes out from the depth of the personality under a disguise that hides the love's presence to the conscious. This 'coming out' of a love or desire allows it to be consummated or fulfilled without the conscious ego knowing about it. And yet the conscious ego experiences the consequences of the love's consummation, which are feelings of pleasure, self-confidence, and well-being.

A second way of thinking about the meaning of dreams is to realize that dreams are caused by other people in the afterlife who are mentally connected with the dreamer. Swedenborg calls them "spirits" and "angels". He presents direct observational evidence of the presence of spirits while he was dreaming. When waking up he could see them standing nearby and talking to each other. He then talked to them and they freely admitted that they caused Swedenborg's dream by what they were talking about.

The topics they discussed were of course spiritual, not natural. All people in the afterlife are no longer able to use a natural language and instead use a spiritual language that is universal and biological to the human race. Swedenborg noted the relationship between the spiritual topics that the spirits discussed and the natural topics in the dream that he could remember.

Still to be explained is how the two conceptualizations of dream content just mentioned are to be reconciled. We need to know the psychological significance of the spiritual topics to the ego-personality's deep structure of affect, love, and desire. What determines what the "spirits" are talking about in relation to the dreamer's personality? When we figure this out we'll be able to know the meaning of dreams. We will also gain a key understanding of fantasy and literature and what significant psychological role they play in human growth.

In Jung's conceptualization it is the psychic forces carried by archetypes that blast the ego-dreamer with content and emotion. There are significant mental risks involved when becoming more spiritual in our thinking and experiencing.

Jung wrote:

> *People may even be destroyed by an archetype, their own existence wiped out forever. In dementia praecox, for instance, it often happens that people are just blasted by an archetype, exploded. They cannot resist it.*

> *If they have an experience which the ordinary religious man would call an experience of God, instead of realizing it as such and thanking heaven for the grace, they think they are God or three times more than God. The archetype has sucked them in and swallowed them. The individual ego is far less resistant; it is futile in comparison.*

> *Therefore the appearance of an archetype in our psychology is always a moment of the greatest danger as well as the greatest hope. ~Carl Jung, Visions Seminar, Page 67*

One must never give way to fear, but one must admit to oneself that one is afraid. ~Carl Jung, C.G. Jung Speaking: Interviews and Encounters, Pages 141-145

Just as the body bears the traces of its phylogenetic development, so also does the human mind. Hence there is nothing surprising about the possibility that the figurative language of dreams is a survival from an archaic mode of thought. ~Carl Jung, General Aspects of Dream Psychology, 1916). In CW 8: The Structure and Dynamics of the Psyche, p. 475

The dream has for the primitive an incomparably higher value than it has for civilized man. Not only does he talk a great deal about his dreams, he also attributes an extraordinary importance to them, so that it often seems as though he were unable to distinguish between them and reality. To the civilized man dreams as a rule appear valueless, though there are some people who attach great significance to certain dreams on account of their weird and impressive character. This peculiarity lends plausibility to the view that dreams are inspirations. ~Carl Jung, The Psychological Foundations of Belief in Spirits, 1920. In CW 8: The Structure and Dynamics of the Psyche, p. .574

To interpret the dream-process as compensatory is in my view entirely consistent with the nature of the biological process in general. Freud's view tends in the same direction, since he too ascribes a compensatory role to dreams in so far as they preserve sleep. ... As against this, we should not overlook the fact that the very dreams which disturb sleep most- and these are not uncommon-have a dramatic structure which aims logically at creating a highly affective situation, and builds it up so efficiently that it unquestionably wakes the dreamer. Freud explains these dreams by saying that the censor was no longer able to suppress the painful affect. It seems to me that this explanation fails to do justice to the facts. Dreams which concern themselves in a very disagreeable manner with the painful experiences and activities of daily life and expose just the most disturbing thoughts with the most painful distinctness are known to everyone. It would, in my opinion, be unjustified to speak here of the dream's sleep-preserving, affect-disguising function. One would have to stand reality on its head to see in these dreams a confirmation of Freud's view. ~Carl Jung, CW 8: The Structure and Dynamics of the Psyche, p. 485

[Visions] are like dreams, only they occur in the waking state. ~Carl Jung, The Psychological Foundations of Belief in Sprits, 1920

"The dream may either repudiate the dreamer in a most painful way, or bolster him up morally. The first is likely to happen to people who ... have too good an opinion of themselves; the second to those whose self-valuation is too low. ~Carl Jung, On the Nature of Dreams, 1945

"The dreams of redemption, whereby God descends into the human realm and man mounts up to the realm of divinity." ~Carl Jung, A Psychological Approach to the Dogma of the Trinity, 1942

Within each one of us there is another whom we do not know. He speaks to us in dreams and tells us how differently he sees us from how we see ourselves. When, therefore, we find ourselves in a difficult situation, to which there is no solution, he can sometimes kindle a light that radically alters our attitude, the very attitude that led us into the difficult situation. ~Carl Jung, Civilization in Transition, 1958

An exclusively sexual interpretation of dreams and fantasies is a shocking violation of the patient's psychological material: infantile-sexual fantasy is by no means the whole story, since the material also contains a creative element, the purpose of which is to shape a way out of the neurosis. ~Carl Jung, The Therapeutic Value of Abreaction, CW 16, par. 277

Dreams are as simple or as complicated as the dreamer is himself, only they are always a little bit ahead of the dreamer's consciousness. I do not understand my own dreams any better than any of you, for they are always somewhat beyond my grasp and I have the same trouble with them as anyone who knows nothing about dream interpretation. Knowledge is *no advantage when it is a matter of one's own dreams. ~Carl Jung, Analytical Psychology, CW 18: p. 122*

I have no theory about dreams; I do not know how dreams arise. And I am not at all sure that - my way of handling dreams even deserves the name of a "method." I share all your prejudices against dream- interpretation as the quintessence of uncertainty and arbitrariness. On the other hand, I know that if we meditate on a dream sufficiently long and thoroughly, if we carry it around with us and turn it over and over, something almost always comes of it. This something is not of course a scientific result to be boasted about or rationalized; but it is an important practical hint which shows the patient what the unconscious is aiming at. Indeed, it ought not to matter to me whether the result of my musings on the dream is scientifically verifiable or tenable; otherwise I am pursuing an ulterior-and therefore autoerotic-aim. I must content myself wholly with the fact that the result means something to the patient and sets his life in motion again. I may allow myself only one criterion for the result of my labors: does it work? As for my scientific hobby-my desire to know why it works-this I must reserve for my spare time. ~Carl Jung, CW 16: The Practice of Self-analysis, p. 86

I leave theory aside as much as possible when analyzing dreams-not entirely, of course, for we always need some theory to make things intelligible. It is on the basis of theory, for instance, that I expect dreams to have a meaning. I cannot prove in every case that this is so, for there are dreams which the doctor and the patient simply do not understand. But I have to make such a hypothesis in order to find courage to deal with dreams at all. ~Carl Jung, CW 16: The Practice of Self-analysis, p. 318

Never apply any theory, but always ask the patient how he feels about his dream images. For dreams are always about a particular problem of the individual about which he has a wrong conscious judgment. The dreams are the reaction to our conscious attitude in the same way that the body reacts when we overeat or do not eat enough or when we ill-treat it in some other way. Dreams are the natural reaction of the self-regulating psychic system. ~Carl Jung, Analytical Psychology, CW 18, p. 123

The view that dreams are merely the imaginary fulfillments of repressed wishes is hopelessly out of date. There are, it is true, dreams which manifestly represent wishes or fears, but what about all the other things? Dreams may contain ineluctable truths, philosophical pronouncements, illusions, wild fantasies, memories, plans, anticipations, irrational experiences, even telepathic visions, and heaven knows what besides.
~Carl Jung, CW 16: The Practice of Self-analysis, p. 317

Once again let me turn back to the fundamental contrast between Freudian and Jungian dream analysis. The essential difference comes from what Freud thought were dreams and what Jung thought and discovered about dreams. We can say what Freud thought of dreams using Jung's words quoted above: "*our ego-consciousness reflecting on itself*". This is precisely what Jung denies and sees as a misconception on the fundamental nature of a dream event. For Jung it became completely evident that a dream is not a personal reflection of the ego reflecting itself to itself, as Freud assumed. Jung discovered the existence and source of dreams in the shared collective unconscious of humankind. This was an objective natural event and property of human minds.

The dream is the place or state in which the ego comes face to face with its "objective actuality". The dream is a "*message from the unconscious*", from the "*unitary soul of humanity*". The message of the dream reflects to the ego consciousness the totality of what the ego is part of. Modern life has led the ego of individuals to materialism and to the "*aberrations of the conscious mind*". These have caused an estrangement from "*the trunk from which the ego grew*" and has turned the unconscious into an "*alien*" and scary phantasm.

We may not be aware of this in our waking state but the dream fantasy continues after the dream is over, after we awaken from sleep and continue our day-to-day activities. We continue our dreaming in waking life "*beneath the threshold of consciousness*". The psychological complexes that the ego represses act continuously when we are sleeping and when we are awake. When awake, the complexes express themselves in abnormal emotions, thoughts, and behaviors. When asleep they express themselves as dreams of various types and content. Jung warns us to take seriously the connection that exists between the two modes of expressing unconscious meanings. The details of a dream may be "*very silly*" and "*producing an impression of absurdity*" that leaves us "*thoroughly bewildered*". Dreams can be "*childish, grotesque, and immoral*".

And yet, when we penetrate the meaning of a dream and its apparently incoherent content, "*we find ourselves deep in the dreamer's secrets and discover with astonishment that an apparently quite senseless dream is in the highest degree significant, and that in reality it speaks only of important and serious matters*". But Jung tells us that the "*art of interpreting dreams cannot be learnt from books*". Dream interpretation is a hazardous attempt that may go off in a mistaken direction and leave the person "*more deeply entangled in mistakes*".

When we dream, a "*little hidden door in the innermost and most secret recesses of the soul, opens into that cosmic night which was psyche long before there was any ego consciousness*". Through that little secret door comes through to us the medicine of recovery by which our artificial life of materialism and reductionism, is healed. The dream door sets up the healing of the ego. The return from the Fall in our civilized evolution. In our prior history as a race, the Fall of the human consciousness brought materialism and the denial of the psychic world as real. The Fall also brought the denial of God as personal, as demanding of us that we suffer ourselves to become heroes through battling and vanquishing the devils that have become part of our anatomy.

Jung wrote that "*all consciousness separates*" which is why dreams restore us to the "*more universal, truer, more eternal man dwelling in the darkness of primordial night*".

> *If one accepts the symbol, it is as if a door opens leading into a new room whose existence one previously did not know. . ~Carl Jung, Liber Novus, p. 311*

The fairy tale is the great mother of the novel, and has even more universal validity than the most-avidly read novel of your time. ~Carl Jung, The Red Book, Page 262.

In early childhood we become acquainted with fairy tales and we learn mythology in school and in our later reading, we forget most of it in consciousness, but in the depths it is all carefully treasured. ~Carl Jung, ETH Lecture, p. 192

Sacred Scripture
or the Word of God

In the modern world today there is no direct revelation of spiritual truths from God, as in most ancient times, or later in the days of prophets. The *Word of God* or *Sacred Scripture* is the only source of spiritual truths. Those who pass into the afterlife without any knowledge of *Sacred Scripture* may have acquired spiritual truths by reading commentaries on *Sacred Scripture* or from lectures and conversations with others who have had access to *Sacred Scripture*. It is therefore necessary for these people to be instructed in the spiritual truths of *Sacred Scripture*. This is done soon after they awaken from the three-day dying-resuscitation process. In this way they can complete their regeneration by undergoing spiritual temptations.

In the following selection Swedenborg is discussing the interaction between people in the afterlife who have not undergone regeneration and arrive in the spiritual world in their natural consciousness, and therefore without an active spiritual consciousness that they can experience. These natural-thinking spirits stalk and obsess those spirits whom they can find who have not yet completed their regeneration and are still vulnerable to spiritual temptations. They therefore are made to serve a useful function to those who are being regenerated by providing them with spiritual temptations.

The reason why they are dangerous, is, because they are able to persuade almost any of the simple and the upright that is or that is to be believed, merely from the external sense of the Word, and without explanation; and the simple have not exerted themselves, and learned, in the world, that the external sense of the Word is according to the apprehension of the sensual man [natural consciousness] - *for the first apprehension of man is sensual; and that this must be the lowest level of the Word, because in the position of a foundation, or in the position of the soles of the feet, whereon the body stands. For the Word is, in the sight of the Lord, like one man; for it is Divine Truth. Hence, the sense of the letter is its sole; but, still, there are interiors corresponding to it, in accordance with the connection of such things as are in man.*
~Swedenborg, Spiritual Experiences 5090

But amongst these are not to be reckoned those, who, owing to immaturity or simplicity, believe the sense of the letter of the Word, and still live according to the doctrine of the Church; but they are those who study the Word, despising the whole of the doctrine from the Word. ~Swedenborg, Spiritual Experiences 5087

Swedenborg's careful analysis of the Old Testament was supplemented by his dual consciousness that allowed him to discover in what way the "Word of God" is addressed simultaneously to all three levels of perfection in human consciousness.

We become at first familiar with the literal historical verses of Sacred Scripture. We are then in natural consciousness and the meaning we comprehend from these literal verses is addressed to life on earth as we experience it in daily life, in education, in history, politics, or science. This is the natural-rational consciousness that is working our mental activity and giving us an interpretation of the meaning of God's sacred text. This is also called "sensual thinking" or "scientific monism" and "materialism".

When we read *Sacred Scripture* in natural-rational consciousness it seems to us that God though the chosen prophets is mostly talking about life in this world. The afterlife is cryptically mentioned here and there, and even this much is portrayed as happening on earth in this world which is to be renewed after the Apocalypse when the dead will be resurrected in their physical body. When it is mentioned that some ancient religious figures died it is not also mentioned that they only died for a few hours and were then resuscitated, continuing their life in the spiritual world of eternity.

The sacred text indicates that when people break God's commandments they are severely punished and all of their punishment consists of bad things *in this world* such as barrenness or the loss of ability to have children, famine in the land, or being killed by the sword and left to be eaten by the vultures. Similarly, nearly all of God's rewards described in the literal sense of the holy text, are portrayed as physical rewards such as riches, jewels, possessions, conquering other nations, large number of offspring, or fertile lands and the products of the earth.

This natural-world history in Sacred Scripture seems to be the bottom level of what God wants to tell us. *It is addressed solely to the human mind when it is operating in natural consciousness.*

When we consider the meaning of the literal verses from the spiritual-rational perspective, everything changes. God is now talking about theistic psychology, human growth, preparation for the afterlife, and spiritual truths of reality. This transformation in message is truly awesome. I have spent more than thirty years studying Swedenborg's details describing this transformation and I still read it with awe and with awareness that I'm only skimming the surface of the unfathomable spiritual depths of God's Word to humanity. And I have the same feeling and awe when I read the Sacred Scriptures of the other major religions and find therein this spiritual-rational level of meaning.

Further, there is a third and highest level of meaning in God's verses and this is called celestial-rational understanding.

The three levels of meaning or truths that are contained in God's Word enter the human mind simultaneously. Every individual's mind receives the three levels of consciousness simultaneously. It is an automatic anatomical process and the individual does not have to be reading Sacred Scripture. The celestial and spiritual levels of meaning are activated by God equally in every living human being anywhere.

People read Sacred Scripture and hear lessons and preaching's about it in their natural consciousness. When they are so exposed they are conscious in the natural mind of God's message. At this level of thinking, the consequences or effects of such knowledge only affect the external ego-personality. God can influence the external ego-personality of individuals by presenting the Word at this level. This is individuation stage 1. Selfishness or love of self is well within the personality and is not affected by such knowledge. The individual cannot be regenerated in this mental state and lifestyle.

Archetypes and Psychology

The unconscious, as the totality of all archetypes, is the deposit of all human experience right back to its remotest beginnings.

Not, indeed, a dead deposit, a sort of abandoned rubbish-heap, but a living system of reactions and aptitudes that determine the individual's life in invisible ways —all the more effective because invisible.

It is not just a gigantic historical prejudice, so to speak, an a priori historical condition; it is also the source of the instincts, for the archetypes are simply the forms which the instincts assume.

From the living fountain of instinct flows everything that is creative; hence the unconscious is not merely conditioned by history, but is the very source of the creative impulse. ~Carl Jung, CW 8, Para 339.

The archetype—let us never forget this—is a psychic organ present in all of us. ~Carl Jung, CW 9i, Para 271

Man must remain conscious of the world of the archetypes, because in it he is still a part of Nature and is connected with his own roots. ~Carl Jung, CW 9i, Para 174

The archetypes are imperishable elements of the unconscious, but they change their shape continually. ~Carl Jung, CW 9i, Para 301

Archetypes are, by definition, factors and motifs that arrange the psychic elements into certain images, characterized as archetypal, but in such a way that they can be recognized only from the effects they produce.

They exist preconsciously, and presumably they form the structural dominants of the psyche in general. They may be compared to the invisible presence of the crystal lattice in a saturated solution.

As a priori conditioning factors they represent a special, psychological instance of the biological "pattern of behaviour," which gives all living organisms their specific qualities.

Just as the manifestations of this biological ground plan may change in the course of development, so also can those of the archetype.

Empirically considered, however, the archetype did not ever come into existence as a phenomenon of organic life, but entered into the picture with life itself. ~Carl Jung, CW 11, Para 222.

It is only through the psyche that we can establish that God acts upon us, but we are unable to distinguish whether these actions emanate from God or from the unconscious. We cannot tell whether God and the unconscious are two different entities. Both are border-line concepts for transcendental contents.

But empirically it can be established, with a sufficient degree of probability, that there is in the unconscious an archetype of wholeness which manifests itself spontaneously in dreams, etc., and a tendency, independent of the conscious will, to relate other archetypes to this centre.

Consequently, it does not seem improbable that the archetype of wholeness occupies as such a central position which approximates it to the God-image. ~Carl Jung, CW 11, Para 757

I am not, however, addressing myself to the happy possessors of faith, but to those many people for whom the light has gone out, the mystery has faded, and God is dead. For most of them there is no going back, and one does not know either whether going back is always the better way. To gain an understanding of religious matters, probably all that is left us today is the psychological approach.

That is why I take these thought-forms that have become historically fixed, try to melt them down again, and pour them into moulds of immediate experience. It is certainly a difficult undertaking to discover connecting links between dogma and immediate experience of psychological archetypes, but a study of natural symbols of the unconscious gives us the necessary raw material. ~Carl Jung, CW 11, Para 148

Religion and Myth

The religious myth is one of man's greatest and most significant achievements, giving him the security and inner strength not to be crushed by the monstrousness of the universe. ~Carl Jung, CW 5, Para 343

Life is never so beautiful as when surrounded by death. ~Carl Jung, 1925 Seminar, p. 85

This remarkable capacity of the human psyche for change, expressed in the transcendent function, is the principal object of late medieval alchemistic philosophy, where it was expressed in terms of alchemical symbolism. ~Carl Jung, CW 7, Para 360

Sometimes people read the above quote, and many similar ones sprinkled throughout Jung's writings, and conclude that Jung considered religion and God as a "mere myth", similar to Freud's idea of religion. But this is an error. Nothing could be further from the truth. As I have shown throughout this book, Jung placed God at the center of his life and of the life of all individuals, though some people are not aware of this relationship they have with God. By declaring that religion is *"man's greatest and most significant achievement"* Jung identified religion with a super-natural existence that is independent of the natural universe. Freud could not fathom this as all his ideas were grounded in materialistic monism. Indeed, Freud's idea of religion as "myth" reduced it to an insignificant function and purely psychological rather than real and actual.

Myth is not fiction: it consists of facts that are continually repeated and can be observed over and over again. It is something that happens to man, and men have mythical fates just as much as the Greek heroes do. ~Carl Jung, CW 11, Para 648

More than once I have had to reach for a book on my shelves, bring down an old alchemist, and show my patient his terrifying fantasy in the form in which it appeared four hundred years ago. ~Carl Jung, CW 13, Para 325

Art is a kind of innate drive that seizes a human being and makes him his instrument. ~Carl Jung, CW 15, Para 157

People associate "mythology" with mere legends and stories originating in pre-modern concepts of reality. According to dictionaries, "Myths are a collection of stories told to explain nature, history, and customs" and appear in all cultures. A myth is said to be an "idealized conception" or a "false belief". This is the sense many people think of. A myth is said to be "*concerning some being or hero or event, with or without a determinable basis of fact*". People learn about Greek mythology and that of other cultures as fiction from ancient times. But Jung's idea was that religion and God are realities anchored in a real and independent psychic existence in the collective unconscious of humanity.

In this respect it is interesting to consider what Swedenborg learned about mythology through his dual consciousness in which he was able to discuss the subject with those in the afterlife who had lived in ancient times.

Religion has existed from the most ancient times, and the inhabitants of the world everywhere have had a knowledge of God, and some knowledge of a life after death. This has not originated from themselves or their own intelligence, but from the Ancient Word mentioned above Nos. 101-103; and in later times from the Israelitish Word. From these two Words forms of religion spread to the Indies and their Islands, through Egypt and Ethiopia to the kingdoms of Africa, from the maritime parts of Asia to Greece, and thence to Italy.

However, as the Word could only be written by representatives, that is, by such things in the world as correspond to and signify heavenly things, therefore religion with many nations was turned into idolatry, and in Greece into mythology. Divine attributes and properties were turned into so many gods, and over these men set one supreme deity whom they called Jove from Jehovah; while it is well known that they had some conception of Paradise, some knowledge of the Flood, the sacred fire, and the four ages from the first or golden age to the last or iron age, by which in the Word are signified the four states of the Church as described in Daniel ii 31-35. It is also known that the Mohammedan religion, which succeeded and destroyed the former religious systems of many nations, was taken from the Word of both Testaments. ~Swedenborg, Doctrine of Sacred Scripture, n. 117

In other words, religion and the idea of God originated from the ancient Sacred Scriptures that spread across the whole world. The "Word" is God's Word, not a legend or false conception sprung from the inventiveness of human beings as found in fiction and literature. It was much later with the decline of spiritual consciousness that religion "*was turned into idolatry*" and hence it was that mythology became mere legend and a collection of stories which were no longer religion but "a ghost of faith" in people's natural consciousness:

Instead there is only a ghost of faith, which from an earthly perspective looks like an image of faith, but from a spiritual perspective looks like a monster from mythology". ~Swedenborg, True Christian Religion TCR 379

The Symbolism of Water

In Jung's words:

In Zimmer's book Maya we find the following passage referring to this: "The waters are the Gegenwelt [counterworld] to the dry sphere of the waking day, into which the eye looks outward; in them the hidden nature of things is mirrored to the inner view. Down into the water means down into knowledge.

The ageless waters, taking all forms of nature, circulating as its life, know everything, they have been present since the beginning and conserve everything in their liveliness—nothing is forgotten.

Thus Vishnu speaks to the holy Naranda: Immerse yourself in water, and you will know about my Maya. The ageless waters, taking all forms of nature, circulating as its life, know everything, they have been present since the beginning and conserve everything in their liveliness—nothing is forgotten.

In another place he writes: The waters of life are the womb of all forms of the world, as well as their grave in which they are reborn, they circulate in and build, they carry and dissolve every form, they are the palpable element of the all divine Maya, whose nature the saints and seers tentatively try to grasp. They hold the secret of this Maya as the force of their own, versatile nature, and do not yield it, but let it be tasted when someone opens up to them. How the world comes into being, every hour, outside as world gestalt in the flow of coming into being and happening, coming to the fore, as gestalt of the inner world, from the dark ness of the unconsciousness into the light of consciousness—all this can be experienced, but how could it be fathomed?

Zimmer also quotes the wondrous motif of someone who immerses himself in water and emerges into a new life, sinking from life dream to life dream in doing so: The cleansing, healing power of the water is also known in Christianity, as the baptismal water that washes away original sin and admits the baptized child into the Church, the Corpus Christi.

The Jews also baptized, and admitted the proselytes into the community. The Gospel of John quotes Christ's words to Nicodemus: "Verily, verily, I say unto thee, Except a man be born again [of water and the spirit], he cannot see the kingdom of God."

Above all, however, we would like to refer to the Revelation of John: "And he shewed me a pure river of water of life, clear as crystal . . . on either side of the river, was there the tree of life, which bare twelve manner of fruits, and yielded her fruit every month" (22:1–2).

"Slowly I am sinking deeper and deeper." This might symbolize a slowly progressing process of being flooded by the unconscious. "I nearly drown" has a parallel in the story about the vision of the snake: "I no longer dare move in the bed, because even when awake, everywhere in the room I see the glowing eyes of the snake that wants to bite me." Her light consciousness of the day is flooded and disturbed by the frightening snake image from the unconscious, so she is deprived of her freedom of movement.

Here, she nearly drowns—the capabilities of her senses are minimized by the unconscious content entering in her ears, nose, and mouth. She is prevented from seeing, hearing, and speaking, and can hardly breathe at all. So she is in an extremely reduced state; there is hardly any possibility left to contact the outer world, life. Psychologically speaking, this could indicate a nearly autistic state, or a very great introversion, which severely restricts the possibilities of her moving or expressing herself.
~Carl Jung, Children's Dreams Seminar, p. 268-272

In Swedenborg's words:

UNLESS A MAN IS BORN AGAIN, AND, AS IT WERE, CREATED ANEW, HE CANNOT ENTER INTO THE KINGDOM OF GOD.
That unless a man is born again he cannot enter into the kingdom of God, is the Lord's doctrine in the following passages from John [New Testament]:

> *Jesus said to Nicodemus, Verily, verily, I say unto thee, Except a man be born anew, he cannot see the kingdom of God; and again, Verily, verily, I say unto thee, except a man be born of water and of spirit, he cannot enter into the kingdom of God; That which is born of flesh is flesh, and that which is born of spirit is spirit (3:3, 5, 6).*

"The kingdom of God" means both heaven and the church, for the church is the kingdom of God on earth. So in other places, where the kingdom of God is mentioned (as in Matt. 11:11; 12:25; 21:43; Luke 4:43; 6:20; 8:1, 10; 9:11, 60, 62; 17:21; and elsewhere).

"To be born of water and the spirit" signifies to be born by means of truths of faith and a life in accordance with them. ... That "spirit" signifies a life in accordance with Divine truths is clear from the Lord's Words in John (6:63). "Verily, verily" [or "Amen, amen"], signifies that this is the truth; and the Lord used that expression so frequently because He was the truth itself. He Himself is also called "the Amen" (Apoc. 3:14). In the Word the regenerate are called "Sons of God" and "born of God," and regeneration is described by "a new heart and a new spirit."
~Swedenborg, True Christian Religion, 572

REGENERATION. He who does not receive spiritual life, that is, who is not begotten anew by the Lord, cannot come into heaven; which the Lord teaches in John:
    Verily, verily, I say unto thee, except anyone be begotten again,
    he cannot see the kingdom of God (3:3).
~Swedenborg, New Jerusalem and Heavenly Doctrine 173

He who has been washed has no need except to wash his feet, so that the whole person is clean. John 13:10. 'He who has been washed' means one who has been regenerated.

The fact that the word 'baptizing' was used to denote the total washing of things is clear in Mark 7:4, and to denote washing the whole body, in Matthew 3:13-16... The Jordan - in which washings, which were baptizings, took place, (Mark 1:5) - meant the natural. Baptismal washing also means temptation (Matt. 20:22, 23); it does so because all regeneration is accomplished by means of temptations.

It must also be stated briefly here why it was that the Lord, when He was in the world, was Himself willing to be baptized, when yet baptism is the sign of a person's regeneration by Him. The reason was that the baptizing of the Lord Himself was a sign of the glorification of His Humanity. Anything in the Word that means a person's regeneration also means the glorification of the Human within the Lord; for a person's regeneration is an image of the Lord's glorification.

This is why the Lord, when He allowed John to baptize Him, said, "Thus it is fitting for us to fulfill all the righteousness of God (Matt. 3:15). 'Fulfilling all the righteousness of God' means subduing the hells, restoring them and the heavens to order, by His own power, and at the same time glorifying His Human.

All this was accomplished by means of the temptations which the Lord allowed Himself to undergo, thus by means of the conflicts with the hells which He underwent repeatedly, even to the last on the Cross. These things constituted the righteousness which the Lord fulfilled. ~Swedenborg, Arcana Coelestia 10239

[Apocalypse] Verse 15. "And the serpent cast out after the woman out of his mouth water as a river", signifies crafty reasonings in abundance respecting justification by faith alone by those who think sensually and not spiritually. This is evident from the signification of a "serpent," as being those who are sensual, and in an abstract sense the sensual, which is the ultimate of the natural in man; ... also from the signification of "the woman," as being the church which will be the New Jerusalem; also from the signification of "mouth," as being thought, from which is speech; also from the signification of "water," as being the truth of faith, and in the contrary sense falsity; also from the signification of "river," as being intelligence from the understanding of the truth, and in the contrary sense reasoning from falsities. ...

Consequently "casting out water as a river" signifies reasoning from falsities in abundance. Keen reasonings respecting justification by faith alone by those who think sensually and not spiritually are here meant, because "the dragon" means those who defend justification by faith alone, and who are sensual, and therefore think and reason sensually and not spiritually.

This is meant for the reason also that "dragons" and "serpents" signify those who are sensual, and because sensual men are more crafty than the rest, and reason keenly from falsities and from fallacies. ... From this it is clear what is signified by the words "the dragon cast out after the woman out of his mouth water as a river." ~Swedenborg, Apocalypse Explained 763

Jung wrote:

If we want to interpret a dream correctly, we need a thorough knowledge of the conscious situation at that moment, because the dream contains its unconscious complement, that is, the material which the conscious situation has constellated in the unconscious. ~Carl Jung, CW 8, Para 477

But when we penetrate the depths of the soul and when we try to understand its mysterious life, we shall discern that death is not a meaningless end, the mere vanishing into nothingness—it is an accomplishment, a ripe fruit on the tree of life. ~Carl Jung, CW 18, Para 1705-7

The archetype is, so to speak, an "eternal" presence, and it is only a question of whether it is perceived by the conscious mind or not. ~Carl Jung, CW 12, Para 329

The principal pair of opposites is the conscious world and the unconscious world, and when the two come together, it is as if man and woman were coming together, the union of the male and the female, of the light and the darkness. Then a birth will take place.
~Carl Jung, Visions Seminar, p. 574

END OF CHAPTER 3

Chapter 4
Swedenborg on Dreams
and the Spiritual World

Due to his continuous dual consciousness for 27 years, Swedenborg was able to go much further than Jung with respect to identifying the psychic forces that cause dreams. Swedenborg was able to look at the source that created the universal archetypes that Jung had discovered. The inmost source or origin creates the interior cause that creates the exterior effect or the dream appearances and details.

Swedenborg held that all successive sequences in creation or creative production appear together at the end effect in simultaneous order. The three systems that make up the mind or spiritual body consist of the affective-circulatory system, which is the inmost; second, the cognitive-respiratory system, which is in between; and finally, the sensorimotor system, which is the outmost or external to the personality.

In other words, when examining the content of dreams we are observing the end effects in the sensorimotor system of some sequence that must have a prior a cause, which is the cognitive system of thoughts, and a still prior source in the personality structure of the sleeper, which is the affective system of loves. Within the end effect or sensorimotor appearance can be found hidden the prior step of the cognitive cause. And within this cause can be seen the prior or first step called the source, which is affective. Another way of saying this is that loves produce thoughts that are translated into scenes.

All three structural components of dreams are united and appear synchronously in the dream content. Thus, the first step after waking up is to remember the external details of the dream content. The second step is to inquire into what these details represent by applying the logic and language of symbolism or correspondences. The third step is to apply this meaning to oneself by trying to identify the love or affect that wants to be fulfilled through the dream. All three steps are united in the dream content.

Dreaming is therefore a process of encoding affect into cognition, and thence into dramatic scenes. The affect or desire is fulfilled in the dream event, which we experience while dreaming. We are not therefore unconscious while sleeping, as it is commonly assumed.

When dreaming we are fully conscious of the dream event at a natural level of consciousness. The dream is produced in our celestial-rational consciousness, which is the inmost. It is elaborated in our spiritual-rational consciousness, which is in the middle. The dream is finally translated into natural-rational consciousness, which is the outmost. This is the level at which we are conscious in our dreaming and can remember when we are awake.

Here is a schematic diagram to explain how the three anatomical systems of the mind and body correspond.

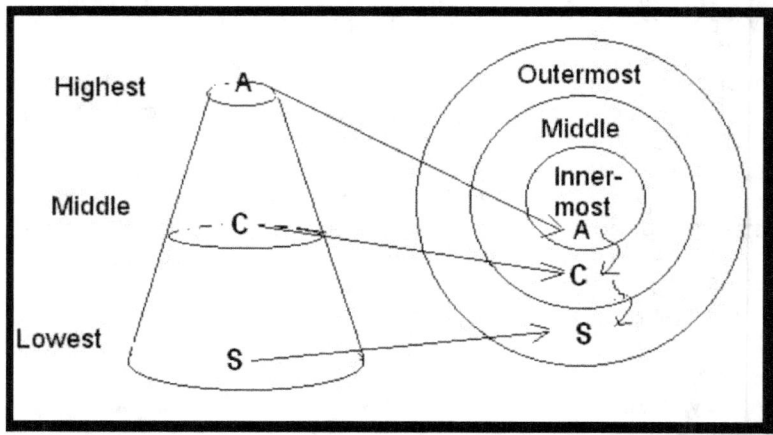

The diagram above shows how the sequential or successive operation in production or encoding (on the left) resolves into simultaneous operation in analysis or decoding (on the right).

When we analyze or decode a dream we start in the reverse direction of its production or encoding. We recall to our mind the dream content in terms of its outmost appearance to a witness, which is the sensorimotor of the dream. This is like a video of the scene that occurs in the dream. This is what we remember after waking up. Clearly, we had to be aware or conscious of the video while it was being played out in dramatic format. The dream video had a witness and a reporter, who is the dreamer or sleeper.

The arrows in the diagram on the right show that the sensorimotor appearance of the video dream was the last operation in production (S), while it is the first in analysis. The right portion of the diagram shows how the three sequential operations in production (on the left) collapse into a horizontal and simultaneous effect in which all three steps are present. But in order to interpret the dream we need to unfold the simultaneous into the sequential, so that we can travel back up to the love (A) that produced the dream (S) through the symbolism of archetypes (C).

When awake we produce the dream report (what happened), images, or other artistic representation in the dream that we can recall. We then unfold or penetrate the dream in depth by analyzing its cognitive content in terms of known objective universal symbolism and correspondences. This gives a partial explanation. It is not complete as it is only the middle step in both production and analysis. The cognitive content or meaning of the dream is not personal but universal. It includes the unconscious archetypes and the universal correspondences between the natural and spiritual worlds. The cognitive element of the dream is merely a vehicle of transmission mediating between the outward sensorimotor appearances and the innermost affective activity that initiated the dream production sequence.

After this we continue the dream interpretation by inquiring in more depth into the innermost aspect of the dream, which is its affective operation. This reveals the unconscious motive, love, intention, or psychological complex that found conscious expression in the dream. It can then be incorporated into the personality structure. This is the therapeutic payoff of dream analysis.

In summary:

The dream production sequence (encoding) proceeds as follows:

affective system (A) → cognitive system (C) → sensorimotor system (S)

The dream analysis sequence (decoding) proceeds in reverse order:

sensorimotor system (S) → cognitive system (C) → affective system (A)

In other words, the three sequential steps in dream *production* are *encoding* operations:

   (1) Some love in the affective system (A) initiates the dream and directs the cognitive system.

(2) The cognitive system (C) supplies an appropriate symbolic expression of that love and activates the sensorimotor system.

(3) The sensorimotor system (S) supplies a natural embodiment that becomes the content of the dream that one remembers.

The three sequential steps in dream *analysis* are *decoding* operations in the reverse direction:

(1) The sensorimotor system (S) that embodied the dream becomes the content of the dream that one remembers and analyzes.

(2) The symbols that were supplied by the cognitive system (C) can now be unfolded, extracted, and identified. This requires familiarity with universal symbolism or correspondences.

(3) The love in the affective system (A) that initiated the dream can then be identified and incorporated into personality structure. This is the therapeutic benefit of self-analysis.

All dreams originate in some particular affective operation that is initiated by the biological psychic tension of the celestial-rational unconscious (A) attempting to descend or externalize into natural-rational consciousness (S) though the intermediary of spiritual-rational consciousness (C) that comprehends universal symbolism and correspondences.

Dreams would not exist without the affective starting point. Loves and emotions are biological psychic forces operating and circulating in the affective-circulatory system of the spiritual body or mind. Loves are arranged in a rank-order hierarchy of precedence or control. Higher loves in rank control the operation of lower loves. In most adults prior to undergoing spiritual regeneration the chief dominant loves of the entire hierarchy are self-love or the love of ruling over others and possessing their wealth and power. This love is inborn from heredity and grows stronger by our own practice or lifestyle. This is the love that must be overcome and neutralized when we are undergoing regeneration or character reformation.

166

Some people say that you have to love yourself before you can love others. This may be a reference to the actual order of development in personality. We love ourselves first during the entire process of maturation from infancy to adulthood. It is important to realize that love of self-only is not merely wanting to take care of our needs and comforts and to pursue our interests. This would be psychologically healthy. But it is not healthy when the love of self becomes exclusively self-centered. This normally happens if the love of self is not informed by conscience and spirituality. Love of self-only progresses and intensifies until only those are loved who benefit and favor us. All others are hated. Hence the love of self always turns into a pathology unless modified by regeneration or individuation.

It is important to understand that the love of self only inhibits and destroys individuation. The love of self is hostile to community and societal institutions, being supportive of them only if they benefit the self. In natural consciousness it is generally not understood that the "love of self" is the same as "the love of self exclusively" or the "love of self alone". In spiritual consciousness it is perceived that the love of self is exclusive and commands a totalitarian function in the personality. This is because our personality is anatomically arranged in an affective hierarchy of loves that dominate and determine what new loves may be acquired or not, and what new ideas and attitudes are admissible to have.

At the very top or very center of the love hierarchy in human consciousness there sits the "ruling love" or chief and ranking love. The ruling love commands all other loves and arranges them in a hierarchy below itself that is consistent and pleasing to it. If the love of self is the ruling love then all other loves will be below it and under its determination. Any show of love for others or any consideration or sympathy shown them, will be conditionally allowed only if it benefits the goals of the love of self. Otherwise the love will be denied, repressed, avoided.

From this anatomical operation you can see that the love of self may be justly called the love of self alone or exclusively.

This anatomical prominence of the love of self alone, or self-love exclusively, is inborn and inherited from parents.

The love of self only is then strengthened and expanded in childhood and adulthood through the addition of many acquired selfish loves that do not take appropriate account of other people whom we affect. This process if not arrested continues uninterrupted until death. Upon resuscitation the personality of the individual is fixed interiorly. *The love hierarchy that was in effect prior to dying remains after resuscitation.* Selfish loves then expel all altruistic or other-directed loves, leaving a biased, irrational and distorted human form that is called a devil or an evil spirit.

All people who share compatible love hierarchies, spontaneously draw toward one another in the afterlife and find themselves living as members of a psychic community that may be described as hellish on the basis of the kind of excessive and insane loves that predominate there. Swedenborg's ethnography of the hells in the afterlife of eternity is quite detailed and gives us amazing information about the sorry state of life for the people there. Certainly this is an experience that we want to avoid!

Since the spontaneous selfish devolution of personality continues if not reversed, *it is most critical for every person to adopt effective counter procedures that arrest the devolution and reverse it.* This is the process of individuation and regeneration.

Consciousness When Dreaming

Swedenborg's dual consciousness, which neither Jung nor Freud possessed, gave him access to the source of dreams.

What he discovered is astonishing, namely, that dreaming involves the cerebrum going to sleep and becoming unconscious, while the cerebellum then awakens and becomes conscious (see Swedenborg, SE 3183; AC 1977). There is a switch in our consciousness or source of sensory input. When we are awake, the cerebellum or new brain is active and aware of our physical and social environment. When we fall asleep we lose awareness of our physical environment as the cerebrum or new brain goes to sleep. The old brain or cerebellum that is asleep when we are awake in daytime, now springs into life at nighttime, awakens, and senses the spiritual environment.

At night when we go to sleep and our cerebellum awakens in consciousness, we are suddenly communicating with the people in the afterlife who specialize in inducing the experience and appearance of dreams. Swedenborg calls them "spirits" because they are in their spiritual body and no longer connected to the physical world. While we are still connected to our physical body, the spirits can see, touch, and interact with our spiritual body, but not with our physical body. The spirits can see that we are asleep by the way our spiritual body looks and behaves, perhaps like we can see a sleepwalker who is not conscious or coherent while walking around in the physical body.

It is worth pointing out here that *we are conscious when we are dreaming*. This may surprise people who assume that sleeping is a state of unconsciousness. *But if we are unconscious during our dreams then how is it that we can remember them?* If we can remember an experience we must have been conscious during the experience. If we can remember our dream then we must have been conscious during the dream. We can thus witness consciously what is happening in the dream. Hence it is that later we can remember what we consciously witnessed while dreaming. The cerebellum being awake during sleeping can thus give us the awareness of the dream while it is happening. Then upon awakening from sleep, the cerebrum that is now awake can give us the memory of the dream.

We are then in a mental state in which the spirits can induce dreams with all the details of appearances that are so intimately familiar to us from nightly dreaming. This is indeed the intimate connection that exists between spirits and people still on earth. This is what I call our *vertical community*. Swedenborg was able to observe how and when the spirits were inducing the dreams in others and in himself. Also, he was able to induce dreams in both spirits and people on earth when he was in a spiritual state of mind afforded by his dual consciousness. The following excerpts not only give us hitherto unknown details about the spiritual process of dreaming, but also gives us details about the spiritual world of the afterlife, thus what each of us can expect when we pass on.

Vertical and Horizontal Consciousness

The nature of consciousness is still little understood in materialistic psychology despite more than two centuries of research and theory. But progress in theistic psychology has brought out this fundamental newly realized fact about consciousness: *The ego is never unconscious.* The ego is always conscious both while asleep and during the three-day dying-resuscitation process. Swedenborg has confirmed this by undergoing this process multiple times, which gave him the empirical observation needed to establish the anatomical fact that consciousness cannot be extinguished. Consciousness is always on, even at death.

It is generally believed that at death our consciousness is like a light that switches off. Even those who are dualists and believe in life after death imagine that we lose our consciousness upon dying until we are resurrected or resuscitated from the death state and then our consciousness switches on again. But Swedenborg's empirical observations prove that even during the process of death we remain conscious. Thousands of people have reported undergoing "near death experiences" in which they remained conscious and were able upon "awakening" to report their experiences during their death or near-death.

This makes sense when you consider that consciousness is a property of the substance of good and truth, which belongs to the Divine Human and is immortal and eternal, always active and living. The consciousness of an individual switches on at birth and never stops to eternity. It is impossible for consciousness to be 'off'.

This new knowledge about death will be very encouraging to many people. Jung frequently urges in his writings and lectures that we need to stop fearing death and dying, and that we need to embrace death as the beginning of our next phase of psychic development and wholeness. Now science is bringing people to that new comforting knowledge and confidence regarding the immortality of our ego-personality. Our consciousness is immortal and death is merely a transition point to a higher and more advanced form of consciousness, life, and love.

The mystery of death is no longer. What humanity on earth has feared for millennia is now repaired. But this is true for only those who wish to think and live in spiritual reality, as Swedenborg states in the following selection. I have added more current expressions in [square brackets] when Swedenborg uses a word that has changed meaning since then or relies on the wider context that is not given in the selection.

> ~Swedenborg, Five Memorable Relations, n. 4-7
> When a man [human being; person] arrives after death in the spiritual world, which generally happens on the third day after he has breathed his last, he seems to himself to be alive as he was in the world, living in a similar house, room and bedroom, with similar dress and clothes, and with similar companions at home. If he was a king or a prince, in a similar court; if a farm labourer, in a similar cottage; the one in countrified, the other in magnificent surroundings. The reason this happens to every person after death is so that death should not seem like death but a continuation of life, and so that the last act of natural life should become the first of spiritual life; and from this he should advance towards his goal, which may be either in heaven or in hell.

After "awakening" from the dying-resuscitation process some "new arrivals" had an exchange with some "angels", who are well-disposed people in the afterlife who assist those who first become cognizant of their spiritual environment. Swedenborg witnessed this resuscitation process being undergone by hundreds of people.

> *On hearing these things the angels say, 'Welcome. We will show you something new, which you have not known or believed before; and this is that every man after death lives in a body just as he did before.' To this the new spirits retort, 'That is impossible; where would he get a body from? Is not his body together with all of him lying dead in the grave?' To this the angels reply with amusement, 'We will give you an ocular demonstration of this', and they say, 'Are you not men in perfect shape! Look at yourselves, feel yourselves; and yet you have left the natural world. The reason why you have so far been unaware of this is that the first state of life after death is exactly similar to the last state of life before death.' On hearing this the new arrivals are amazed, and in heartfelt joy exclaim, 'Thanks be to God that we are alive and death has not utterly destroyed us.' I have often heard newcomers taught about their life beyond the grave in this way and delighted at their own resurrection.*

It may be of interest here to read what Swedenborg has written about what people could discover on their own about life after death, especially those who could read Sacred Scripture in its spiritual sense, not just natural-historical. Swedenborg enumerates seven *"things which they might have known of themselves had they chosen to use their reason"*:

> *~Swedenborg, Heavenly Secrets, AC 3957*
> *I have been permitted to speak on this subject with very many in the other life who were from the Christian world, and with the more learned also [philosophers and scientists]; but wonderful to say, scarcely anyone of those with whom I have been permitted to speak knew anything about it, when yet they might of themselves have known much about such things if they had only been willing to use their reason. But as they had not been solicitous about the life after death, but only about life in the world, such things had no interest for them.*

It is worth noting here that nothing has changed over the 270 years since Swedenborg wrote that statement. For the past several generations, people have gone through state supported mandatory public schools where the teachers and the textbooks have promoted materialistic science as the only sane and intelligent approach to understanding reality. Thus it is that for many people today life after death seems like a fantasy, when in fact it is the reality. Materialistic science and public education is therefore immersed and sourced in deep un-reality.

The things which they might have known of themselves had they chosen to use their reason, are the following:

First, that when man [human being; person] is divested of his [physical] body, he comes into the full exercise of a much more enlightened understanding than when living in the body, for the reason that while he is in the [physical] body, corporeal and worldly things occupy his thoughts [materialistic thinking], which induce obscurity [in reasoning; understanding]; but when he is divested of the body, such things do not interfere, and it is with him as with those who are in interior thought by abstraction of the mind from the things of the outward senses [scientific dualism].

From this they might know that the state after death is much more clear-sighted and enlightened than the state before death; and that when a man dies, he passes comparatively [in understanding] from shade into light, because he passes from the things of the [physical] world to those of heaven [spiritual world], and from the things of the [physical] body to those of the spirit [spirit body].

But wonderful to say, although they are able to understand all this, they nevertheless think the contrary, namely, that the state of life in the [physical] body is relatively clear, and that the state of life after being divested of the [physical] body is relatively obscure.

In other words, when people "awaken" from the dying-resuscitation process they still think in the same consciousness modality as they did prior to dying. The un-reality of materialism does not disappear in the reality of the afterlife. This is what Swedenborg calls "spiritual insanity". The psychological harm produced by the un-reality of materialism continues its toll into the personality of the afterlife. *This should alert people to the enormous consequences of uncritically continuing in the school-instilled materialistic consciousness even after reaching adulthood.*

Continuing with Swedenborg's enumeration of the consequences of remaining materialistic until the end:

> *The Second thing that they may know if they will use their reason, is that the life which man has procured for himself in the [physical] world follows him; that is, he is in such a life after death. For they may know that without dying altogether no one can put off the life which he has acquired from infancy; and that this life cannot be changed into another in a moment, still less into an opposite one.*

> *For example: he who has acquired a life of deceit, and has found in this the delight of his life, cannot put off the life of deceit, but is still in that life after death. He who is in the love of self, and thereby in hatred and revenge against those who do not serve him, and those who are in other such evils, remains in them after the life of the [physical] body; for these are the things which they love, and which constitute the delights of their life, and consequently their veriest life; and therefore such things cannot be taken away from them without at the same time extinguishing all their life. And so in other cases.*

In other words, it is not rational to imagine that in the afterlife our personality is different from what it is before we die. Our ego-personality is an accumulated organic structure that has grown and developed into what it is through our lifestyle habits of thinking, emoting, speaking, and behaving. If this ego consciousness is altered drastically into a different personality, different way of thinking and emoting, would you feel yourself? Or would you feel as having been hijacked by somebody else? Hence the saying of the ancients, *Where the tree falls, there it lies*. The *tree* represents our ego-personality or consciousness. *Falling* represents dying. In other words, after resuscitation from death our personality is not different from before.

> *The Third thing which a man may know of himself, is that when he passes*

174

into the other life he leaves many things behind which have no place there, such as cares for food, for clothing, for a place of abode, and also for gaining money and wealth, as well as for being exalted to dignities, all of which are so much thought of by man in the life of the body; but in the other life are succeeded by others that are not of this earthly kingdom.

In other words, to prepare ourselves adequately for life after death we ought to consider what kind of life we will have in the afterlife of the spiritual world. There are many wonderful children stories about life in heaven with the angels that show that life is different there. It is more of a magical environment when people and buildings appear and disappear instantaneously, and where a wish has immediately powerful consequences in reality. But especially through the experience of dreaming, people can realize that the spiritual world is a mental world in which the individual creates the environment and the events in accordance with one's wishes or loves. Hence there are no jobs to hold down or money to possess in order to have what one wants.

Therefore the Fourth thing a man can know is that he who in the world has thought solely of such worldly things, so that he has been wholly possessed by them, and has acquired delight of life in them alone, is not fitted to be among those whose delight is to think about heavenly things, that is, about the things of heaven.

The "things of heaven" are the things of love and truth, while the things of earth or "worldly" things are those of power and riches. Let Swedenborg's eye-witness report stand as a warning message to those who adopt the materialistic habit of thinking and saying that stone and money are real because you can touch them and they have power, while thoughts and loves are not real because they are just "in your head". A castle of stone is considered real, but a castle you imagine is not real, "it is just in your head". And yet there are many in history who wrote and taught that "ideas are stronger than arms". And those familiar with psychology know that a person's attitude is a powerful determinant of perception and of decision-making.

Hence for the sake of our afterlife we need to develop dualist and theistic thinking that will allow us to adapt to the new reality conditions of life in a mental or psychic world where the mind and consciousness are the forces of power that make everything happen, and where physical power and objects are figments of insanity. *The enormous consequence of such insanity is to have to live in a mental hell forever.*

> *From this follows also a Fifth thing; namely, that when the externals of the body and the world are taken away, the man is then such as he has been inwardly; that is, he so thinks and so wills. If his thoughts have inwardly been deceits, machinations, aspiration for dignities, for gains, and for fame thereby; if they have been hatreds and revenges and the like, it can be seen that he will still think such things, thus the things that belong to hell, however much he might for the sake of the before-mentioned ends have concealed his thoughts from men, and thus appeared outwardly to be worthy, while leading others to believe that he had not such things at heart. That all such externals, or simulations of worth, are also taken away in the other life, may likewise be known from the fact that outward things are put off together with the body, and are no longer of any use. From this everyone may conclude for himself what kind of a man he will then appear to the angels* [social life with others].

In other words, in the afterlife we continue to think and will those things that we did in the natural world, but now we are no longer in a physical world. Physical objects, possessions, and positions of power cannot exist in a purely mental world such as is the afterlife of eternity where mental is substance while physical is nothing. Now what you think and love determine what happens around you. If in this life you think deceits and hatreds for the sake of gaining advantage or fame, then you will continue to do so in the afterlife where there is no advantage over others or fame and dignities of power and influence. You are therefore left with nothing but fantasies of dignities, fame, and power which your deceits and hatreds fail to bring you. Instead, these bring insanity and inability to adapt to reality. And these are the "things of hell", thus of a life of suffering and madness.

The Sixth thing that may be known is that heaven, or the Lord through heaven, is continually working and inflowing with good and truth; and that if there is not then in men--in their interior man which lives after the death of the body--some recipient of good and truth, as a ground or plane, the good and truth that flow in cannot be received; and for this reason man while living in the body ought to be solicitous to procure such a plane within himself; but this cannot be procured except by thinking what is good toward the neighbor, and by willing what is good to him, and therefore doing what is good to him, and thus by acquiring the delight of life in such things. This plane is acquired by means of charity toward the neighbor, that is, by means of mutual love; and is what is called conscience. Into this plane the good and truth from the Lord can inflow, and be received therein; but not where there is no charity, and consequently no conscience; for there the inflowing good and truth pass through, and are turned into evil and falsity.

Again Swedenborg warns us that "*while living in the* [physical] *body we ought to be solicitous to procure such a plane within ourselves*". This is the "plane" of reality within our consciousness that is composed of heavenly things, which are the things of mutual love and love of God. This is the ego-personality with which we can strive in eternal happiness. Materialistic thinking loves self more than others. It makes no sense to love others as much as self, and seems insane to love others more than self.

But this materialistic philosophy is the life of hell, whereas the life of heaven is to love others as much or more than self, and to love self more than others is considered insane and opposed to spiritual reality. Individuation and regeneration are therefore essential activities we must take on in our daily life here on earth. When we love others as much as self or more so, then good and truth-substance flows into our personality and activates our spiritual consciousness. But when we love ourselves more than others this inflow is blocked and turned into its opposites. Hence is the life of hell.

The Seventh thing that a man can know of himself, is that love to God and love toward the neighbor are what make man to be man, distinct from brute animals; and that they constitute heavenly life, or heaven; while their opposites constitute infernal life, or hell. But the reason why a man does not know these things is that he does not desire to know them, because he lives the opposite life, and also because he does not believe in the life after death; and likewise because he has taken up with principles of faith, but none of charity; and consequently believes in accordance with the doctrinal teachings of many, that if there is a life after death, he can be saved by faith, no matter how he has lived, even if his faith is received in his dying hour. ~Swedenborg, Heavenly Secrets, AC 3957

Swedenborg's Correspondences and Jung's Archetypes

The scarab is a classical rebirth symbol. According to the description in the ancient Egyptian book Am-Tuat, the dead sun God transforms himself at the tenth station into Khepri, the scarab, and as such mounts the barge at the twelfth station, which raises the rejuvenated sun into the morning sky. ~Carl Jung, Synchronicity as a Principle of Acausal Connection, 1952, CW 8, §843

The "Anch"
Symbol of Regeneration and Spiritual Life.

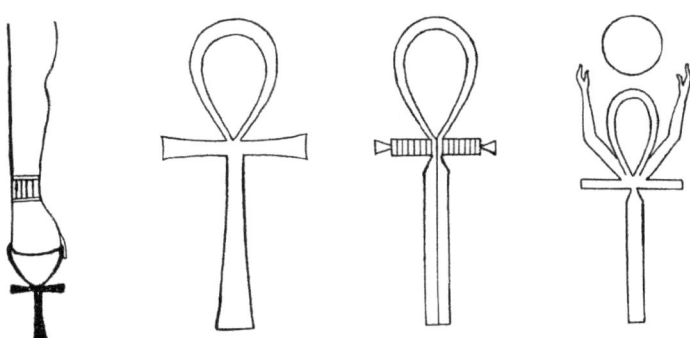

In 1914 C. T. Odhner published a book that explored the application of Swedenborg's correspondences to Egyptian, Greek, and Roman myths. This is a most fortunate and useful work that has been posted on the Web. I recommend it to readers who wish to explore symbolism. The contents of the book are relevant to the thinking of Jung and Swedenborg on sacred symbols and correspondences. It is clear from this work that Jung's archetypal symbols of religion and the collective unconscious are closely related to Swedenborg's correspondences between natural and spiritual things.

Odhner writes about the "anch" symbol that is related to the Christian symbol of the Cross:

> *Of all the symbols of the Egyptians, the one most frequently seen is the peculiar cross which is known as the "anch" or "crux anchata," -- formed by the combination of a cross and a loop which was, perhaps, originally a circle. Almost every Egyptian divinity carries the "anch" in one of his hands, while with the other he grasps the long staff or scepter, known as the "tcham." The rays proceeding from aten, the god of the solar disk, terminate in hands, each of which extends an "anch" to the worshippers. The resurrected spirit is often represented as rising out of the sepulchre, holding an "anch" in each hand, and on his final entrance into "Amenti" or Heaven, the justified spirit is again presented with the "anch" and the staff, as the symbols of eternal life and spiritual power of progress and usefulness.*

> *While all Egyptologists admit that they do not know the origin of this symbol, or what natural object it represents, they unanimously declare that it signifies life, and especially life after death, eternal life. The reason for this signification they do not profess to know, but they tell us that the earliest Christians in Egypt adopted it as the symbol of the crucifixion, and it is frequently found on the Christian monuments in Egypt.*

> *To a Newchurchman* [followers of Swedenborg] *this interesting symbol suggests many things, -- most obviously the crown of eternal life which is won by the cross of temptations. The signification of the cross, as*

meaning temptation, suffering, and death, was known to the Ancient Church throughout the world, long before the crucifixion of the Lord made it the most sacred emblem of the Christian faith. Its very form suggests at once the idea of the self-will of man, (the downward stroke), being broken by the level stroke of rational truth, the experience, when successful, resulting in the circle of eternal happiness.

The "anch" was represented in various elaborate forms, and in the book of the dead it is often provided with a pair of human arms and legs. In Fig. 3 (Plate i) of our illustrations the "anch" clearly represents the regenerated human soul, with delicate arms raised in adoration of the heavenly Sun. To us this simple symbol is full of tender and touching religious affection.

Odhner also explores various other religious symbols of the ancients including staffs and scepters carried by kings, crowns and headdresses, the Tet-pillar or tree of degrees that relates to the Tree of Life in the Old Testament. Odhner specifies the connection in symbolism between the Egyptian symbols and Christian representations of Christ as the incarnated God-Man:

It is to be noted that the "tet" is always and exclusively the symbol of osiris, the God-man, who was born on earth, who blessed mankind with his wise teachings and beneficent rule, who was treacherously slain by the power of evil, but arose after death in his whole human but glorified body, to reign henceforth as the Divine Judge of the other world. Hence we often find the "tet" represented in the form of the mummied body of Osiris, holding the flagellum and the shepherd's crook.

Other well known "*conventionalized emblems*" include the "*symbolic eye*" seen in amulets and necklaces that were worn for good luck.

The "symbolic eye," called "utat or "utchat," is one of the most common of the symbols and is frequently found as an amulet made of glazed faience, wood, precious stones, silver, or gold, Whole necklaces, made of nothing but these eyes, were wrapped around the mummies within and also outside the cloth wrapping, and in the inscriptions the eye was placed wherever the emblem of "understanding" seemed appropriate.

Sometimes it was furnished with a pair of wings, or wings and legs, or with a pair of arms in a worshipping attitude (Fig. 3), or holding the "anch" in the hands. It is usually seen as a single eye, either the left or the right, but very often both eyes are represented, and sometimes it is seen in triple or quadruple forms.

It was a most popular amulet, as its possession was supposed to confer safety and happiness under the protection of the all-seeing eye of God, and as a word the "utat" or "utchat" means "good health, safety and happiness.

With his dual consciousness Swedenborg was able to explore by direct observation the religious symbols of the ancient peoples who lived on earth thousands of years ago and whom Swedenborg was able to visit and interview for his reports and experiments in the spiritual world.

In the following selection, Swedenborg reports that the symbolism of the "most ancient peoples" was at once religious and scientific. It was scientific because their dual consciousness, like that of Swedenborg, allowed them direct observational evidence of the spiritual world and that it is the world of the afterlife where their family and people can be rejoined at death.

They were able to confirm that the spiritual world of the afterlife is actually the mental world so familiar to all of us, and that it is substantive and without fixed time, space, or matter. We are all familiar with our stupendous ability of producing in our dreams and in fantasies anything we know of or can imagine. To our dream avatar, that is to our asleep but conscious ego, the spaces, objects, and times we construct appear real, and are real. That is, they are substantive. So the most ancients studied the cause-effect connection between the spiritual or mental and the physical. They called this the "science of correspondences".

This shows then how the symbolism of the most ancients was scientific because they were actual correspondences that had to be empirically observed. But this symbolism was also religious, as Jung noted and confirmed through his studies of comparative religion. The religious symbolism of correspondences was considered most holy by these ancient cultures. This was on account of the fact that their Sacred

Scripture, which was an oral tradition in pre-literate times, was given to them in correspondences that matched their dual consciousness.

The literal verses of their Holy Oral Text was written in a style appropriate for the natural consciousness in which they managed their physical avatar in their daily lives on earth. This literal text consisted of made up histories that delighted their children and themselves. This made it easy for them to memorize the text and to present it to children and those who were not inclined to scholarly analysis of their Text.

Their knowledge of correspondences allowed them to discover the anatomical and substantive relationship between their natural-consciousness that delighted in the Holy Text's made-up stories on the one hand, and on the other, their spiritual consciousness and meaning that they accessed through their knowledge of correspondences. They constructed religious doctrines for their faith and worship as guides or Divine Commandments regarding how they are to live.

The science of correspondences was the oldest science in human history. Of course most of us are taught that science is a modern invention and practice, while the ancients were "pre-modern", "pre-scientific", and "primitive" cultures. But this is an error. The pre-scientific or primitive cultures existed much later than the most ancient peoples who had an advanced religious and scientific tradition. But note well: this refers to their *spiritual*-rational science, not *natural*-rational science, which indeed started in the modern era following the anti-scientific cultures of the middle-ages.

Jung was a unique giant of the 20th century modern scientific era. He alone among important modern scientists was able to discover that natural-rational science of modern times is spiritually ignorant and insane. Modern science does not know anything about the psychic world and the spiritual world of the afterlife, nor about the science of correspondences or the symbolism of archetype that causally connect the two worlds, psychic and physical.

Jung therefore warned humanity that modern materialistic science has put society in a most dangerous situation by inviting the attack of the frightening dark forces of humanity's collective unconscious. The modern scientific era has unleashed weapons of mass destruction and the daily psychopathologies of criminality, depression, and repressed potential.

Rational theistic thinking can heal this spiritual insanity and allow science to leap forward to scientific dualism and spiritual reality.

Swedenborg writes:

> The reason why the idolatrous practices of the gentiles in antiquity originated from the science of correspondences was that everything to be seen on earth has a corresponding meaning; this is true not only of trees, but also animals and birds of every kind, as well as fish and other things.

> The ancient people who possessed the science of correspondences made themselves images to correspond to heavenly ideas; and they took pleasure in them because they stood for such things as concern heaven and the church. They placed these images therefore not only in their temples, but also in their houses, not so as to worship them, but to call to mind the heavenly ideas they stood for.

> Hence it was that in Egypt and elsewhere they used images of calves, oxen and snakes, not to mention children, old men and young women. Calves and oxen meant the affections and powers of the natural man, snakes the prudence and craftiness of the man who relies upon his senses. Children meant innocence and charity, old men wisdom, young women affections for truth, and so on.

> Once the knowledge of correspondences had been wiped out, their descendants started to worship as holy, and finally as deities, the images and statues their ancestors had erected, because they were in or near temples. This too was the reason why the ancients worshipped in gardens and plantations, depending on the species of tree, as well as on mountains and hills. Gardens and plantations meant wisdom and intelligence, and each tree meant some particular detail of them. For instance, the olive meant the good of love, the vine truth coming from that good, the cedar rational good and truth; a mountain meant the highest heaven and a hill the heaven below this.

> The fact that the science of correspondences was preserved among a number of eastern peoples right down to the Lord's coming can be

established by the wise men from the east, who came to visit the Lord at the time of His birth; therefore the star went before them, and they brought gifts with them, gold, frankincense and myrrh (Matt. 2:1, 2, 9-11). The star which went before them meant knowledge learned from heaven, gold celestial good, frankincense spiritual good, and myrrh natural good; it is these three kinds of good which are the source of all worship. Nonetheless correspondences were totally unknown to the Israelite and Jewish people, even though all the details of their worship, all their laws and judgments given them by Moses, and everything in the Word were nothing but correspondences. ~Swedenborg, True Christian Religion, 205

Indubitably resurrection is one of the most—if not the most—important item in the myth or the biography of Christ and in the history of the primitive church. ~Carl Jung, The Symbolic Life, p. 692

Jung studied religious symbols across the world and discovered their psychological significance referring to them as "archetypes" that existed in the collective unconscious of humanity. The psychological function of universal archetypes is to facilitate the interaction between the conscious and the unconscious. These archetypes are accessible through dreams, art, and literature. Swedenborg was able to observe how these archetypes enter the sleeper's mind through the facilitation of "spirits" who are in active in the collective unconscious.

Jung wrote:

What is very important is to exist, and that's rarer than one realizes. To have a daily task and to accomplish it; and at the same time to attend to what is going on, inside oneself as well as outside, conscious of all life's forms, all its expressions.

... I have no system, no doctrine, nothing of that kind. I am an empiricist, with no metaphysical views at all. ... There is the self, which is the totality of one's being, known and unknown, conscious and unconscious, as opposed to the distinction between physical and psychic.

Then there are the archetypes, those images of instinct. For instinct is not just an outward thrust, it also takes part in the representation of forms. The animal, for example, has a certain idea of the plant, since he recognizes it.

Our instincts do not express themselves only in our actions and reactions, but also in the way we formulate what we imagine. Instinct is not only biological, it is also, you might say, spiritual.

And it always repeats certain forms which can be studied down the ages among all peoples. These are the archetypes. The crossing of a river, now, that is an archetypal situation. It's an important moment, a risk. There is danger in the water, on the banks.

... I remember river crossings in Africa with crocodiles, and unknown tribes on the other side; one feels that one's destiny —human destiny, almost—is at stake. Every man has his own way of approaching the crossing, you see.

... There is also the collective unconscious, that immense treasury, that great reservoir, whence mankind draws the images, the forces, which it translates into very different languages, but whose common source is being found out more clearly all the time. ~Carl Jung, C.G. Jung Speaking: Interviews and Encounters, p. 410-423

For our spirit has become an impertinent whore, a slave to words created by men and no longer the divine word itself. ~Carl Jung, Liber Novus, p. 300

Symbol-formation, therefore, must obviously be an extremely important biological function. ~Carl Jung, CW 6, Para 402

Is there a suffering that would be too great to want to undergo for our God? ~Carl Jung, Liber Novus, p. 300

And if you lose yourself in the crowd, in the whole of humanity, you also never arrive at yourself; just as you can get lost in your isolation, you can also get lost in utter abandonment to the crowd. ~Carl Jung, Zarathustra Seminar, p. 1020

Christianity, like every closed system of religion, has an undoubted tendency to suppress the unconscious in the individual as much as possible, thus paralyzing his fantasy activity.

Instead, religion offers stereotyped symbolic concepts that are meant to take the place of his unconscious once and for all. The symbolic concepts of all religions are recreations of unconscious processes in a typical, universally binding form. Religious teaching supplies, as it were, the final information about the "last things" and the world beyond human consciousness.

The forms welling up from his unconscious are declared to be universally valid and thus replace the individual fantasies of others. ~Carl Jung, CW 6, Para 80

Heaven is wishing better for others than for ourselves with all our heart and serving others for the sake of their own happiness, not for any selfish goal but for love. ~Swedenborg, Secrets of Heaven, AC 452

How And By Whom
Dreams Are Produced

In the following selections Swedenborg is describing his dreaming while being in dual consciousness so that he could afterwards upon awakening interview the spirits and angels that induced his dreams by the use of representations, correspondences, and role-play performances.

People in the afterlife are called spirits and angels. It is not generally known that spirits and angels are closely connected to people still on earth. Swedenborg confirms that if spirits and angels were removed from influx into our mind we would not be able to think anything when we are awake, or have dreams when asleep. Every one is connected to both good spirits and evil spirits so that the individual may be in balance between altruistic and selfish loves.

After awakening from the two-say dying-resuscitation process we are at first spirits and we continue to sleep and have dreams. Swedenborg noted that the content of dreams with spirits is often therapeutic and accordingly directed by God. Good spirits induce pleasant dreams while evil spirits induce frightening and distressing dreams.

Dreams can be induced by representations or by role-playing in which each spirits takes on a role and performs it in the dream. Swedenborg was able after awakening to talk to each spirit and the role they played. Spirits are able to access the sleeper's memory, which they use to make the role-play to seem realistic and convincing to the sleeper.

How Dreams Are Produced

I have learned by much experience, how dreams are produced, and what spirits produce them. When in a state of wakefulness, and when another [was] in a state of sleep, or in sleep, I was then as it were a spirit in company with spirits: and thus it was granted to me to be present with those spirits who introduce dreams, and it was also granted me to introduce dreams; and that it was so I have learned from experience, inasmuch as another waked up, three or four times, after dreams were introduced by me, and I then related the things [of his dream] which he acknowledged. It was granted me to introduce such things as were delightful and pleasant.

I was then instructed by living experience, who they were that introduced dreams and how. It occurred by means of representations, for the end that the sleeper might be delighted, and there are those whose office it is to watch over man, when he sleeps, that he may not be infested by evil spirits. They discharge this office in wakefulness with the greatest delight, so that they strive which of them may be present; and because they are good spirits, they love those things which are most pleasant and delightful to those [asleep]. ~Swedenborg, Spiritual Experiences 3181

About spirits of different kinds, and their plays. This past night I also observed that there were spirits who presented dreams, and that their life was dreams, while a person is sleeping. When several persons are dreamt of, each spirit plays the role of one person - a fact that I openly discovered upon awakening, for then I spoke quite a while with those who were acting the part of this or that person. The evil spirits' fantasies are foreboding and cruel, as they delight in treating people cruelly. So that I would realize this, their savageness continued for a long time after I awoke, and they could not desist from it. ~Swedenborg, Spiritual Experiences 3181

Concerning dreams. During the night I dreamt, and when I awoke I spoke with two who [appeared] in the dream, who acknowledged that they were the ones; and afterwards with a certain angelic spirit into whom, when in the state of sleep, something was apperceived to flow from the Lord, which he also confessed. It thence appeared that dreams are of a two-fold kind; one flows in from spirits, who act [the part of] the persons that are seen in the dreams, and precisely as the dreaming appearance is; the other kind, of which we have spoken before, consists of things introduced by those who are in front above, and by others, which are usually representations, and though persons are in like manner introduced, yet they are merely representations of them. A third kind is from the Lord mediately or immediately through heaven. - 1748, November 6. ~Swedenborg, Spiritual Experiences 3877

To make me fully aware of the way that dreams flow in I was put to sleep and dreamt of a boat approaching that was laden with delicacies and savories of every kind. These were stowed away in the boat, out of sight. On deck stood two armed guards, as well as a third man who was the captain. The boat was passing by into a kind of arched dock; and with this I woke up and thought about the dream. At that point the angelic spirits in front and above me over to the right addressed me. They declared that they were the source of this dream. So that I would know for sure that they were the source of it I was brought into a state where I was so to speak both asleep and awake at one and the same time.

In a similar way they introduced different things that were pleasing and delightful, for example, an unknown tiny creature which was transformed into an object with blackish and shining rays which shot into my left eye at a fantastic speed. They also presented human beings, and also small children variously adorned, and other things besides whose delightfulness was indescribable. I spoke to those angelic spirits about these things also. This took place not just once but on a number of occasions, and each time they taught me by word of mouth. ~Swedenborg, Arcana Coelestia 1977

After such dreams I have very frequently been permitted to speak with the spirits and angels who had introduced them; and they told what they had introduced, and I what I had seen. But it would be too tedious to relate all my experience of these matters. ~Swedenborg, Arcana Coelestia 1979

I may relate one more instance of a similar kind. I dreamed a dream, but a common one. When I awoke, I related it all from beginning to end. The angels said that it coincided exactly with what they had spoken of together; not that the things seen in the dream were the same, for they were wholly different, being things into which the thoughts of their conversation were turned, but in such a way that they were representative and correspondent; and this in every particular, so that nothing was wanting.

I then spoke with them about influx, as to how such things flow in and are varied. There was a person of whom I had the idea that he was in natural truth, which idea I had gathered from the acts of his life. There was a conversation among the angels about natural truth, and on this account that person was represented to me; and the things he said to me, and did, in my dream, followed in order representatively and correspondently from the discourse of the angels with one another. But still there was nothing precisely alike, or the same. ~Swedenborg, Arcana Coelestia 1981

Moreover there was another, who in the life of the body, thought ill of me, as I apperceived, because he spoke thereof so that if it had been allowed he would have persecuted me to death; such was his purpose, and it was discovered that he would have killed me. He was also in a dream, and then was his dream represented to me, whereby was discovered how something had occurred, and how he had attempted connection with a virgin in a privy. Thus also may those things be manifestedly disclosed with all the circumstances, places and persons which [occurred] in the life of the body, [and] which they had done. ~Swedenborg, Spiritual Experiences 3883

Spirits Also Have Dreams

Some, due to a special mercy, are prepared by means of deep sleep, and in the sleep by troubling dreams. There was also one who kept on saying only, "I am silent," and "I am speaking," and this quite frequently. Upon being asked what this was, he gave no other reply. But I heard from others that he had been let into sleep, and I was taught that some are let into these sleeps and undergo purgings by means of dreams, perhaps also by short awakenings, until they are rid of the fantasies they had carried with them. 1747, the 30th day of December. ~Swedenborg, Spiritual Experiences 427

When I awoke I thought about the dream, and then began to speak with those who introduced dreams, who were above me, a little to the front.

They spoke and said that they introduced everything, but I perceived that [my dream came] through them from angelic spirits, who were near that region where paradises appear, and that they showed me [those things]; they also showed me many things when awake, which they introduced into others, to wit, into spirits who slept, with whom I then spoke, and they acknowledged it.

I then saw those things which they introduced, which were so delightful and varied, such inexpressible delights, and also men and infants so adorned that they can never be described; besides in the beginning a sort of unknown animalcule, which dispersed like black rays, they wonderfully spread around the left eye; besides other things which I do not remember. There pertained to the spirits inducing dreams, a certain loud [sonorous] sound, as if the song of certain at a distance, ended obscurely in a sound similar to so [loud] a sound. They also said that they could induce sleep whenever they pleased; which also as I believe they did effect. ~Swedenborg, Spiritual Experiences 3381

Concerning Various Kinds Of Spirits And Their Sports

This night I also observed that there were spirits who represented dreams, and that this was their life whilst man is asleep; and that when many persons are dreamed of, each of those spirits took the role of one person. I manifestly discovered this when I awoke, for I then spoke for quite a time with those who acted the part of this or that person. The phantasies of evil spirits are dire and cruel, the spirits taking delight in cruelly treating men; in order that I might perceive this, their savagery was continued for some time after I awoke, nor could they desist. ~Swedenborg, Spiritual Experiences 180

Spirits also sleep. Last night there were many spirits around me, about someone or several of whom I spoke in the morning, and I heard that they had been sleeping, and in fact pleasantly, as I also perceived. So sleep is also a state proper to spirits, as it is to people on earth. When I was nearly awake but before I woke up, various lights appeared to me, something bright having glittering bubbles, something darker, then something colored. I was told that there are lights like these in their sleep, with variety. And I also realized that they too had had dreams, and pleasant ones, without my having had dreams at the same time. For it is known that when a person on earth is in their company, the person has dreams together with them, spoken of several times [7, 1882]; but in this instance they had dreams, and I had not. 1748, 30 June. ~Swedenborg, Spiritual Experiences 2436

The Dreams of Prophets

It is known from the Word that there was an influx from the world of spirits and from heaven into the prophets, partly by dreams, partly by visions, and partly by speech; and also with some into the very speech and into the very gestures, thus into the things that belong to the body; and that at the time they did not speak from themselves, nor act from themselves, but from the spirits who were then in possession of their bodies. At such times some of them behaved like insane persons, as did Saul when he lay naked; others when they wounded themselves; others when they put horns on themselves, and others in similar ways. ~Swedenborg, Arcana Coelestia 6212

And as I longed to know in what manner these men were actuated by spirits, I was shown by means of a living experience. To this end I was for a whole night possessed by spirits, who so took possession of my bodily things that I had only a very obscure sensation that it was my own body. When these spirits came, they appeared like little clouds heaped together into various forms, for the most part pointed; the little clouds were black. In the morning I saw a chariot with a pair of horses, in which a man was being conveyed. Afterward I saw a horse on which someone was sitting, who was thrown off from the horse backward, and there lay while the horse was kicking. Afterward another was seen seated on a horse. They were noble horses. ~Swedenborg, Arcana Coelestia 6212

After these things were seen, the angels told me what they signified, namely, that the chariot in which the man was, signified the spiritual sense that was in the prophetical things that were uttered, and which these represented; that the horse which threw his rider and kicked, signified the Jewish and Israelitish people with whom were these things, that people being solely in externals, and therefore the intellectual rejected them, and as it were by kicking put them away; and that the other sitting on the horse signified the intellectual with those who are in the internal sense of the prophetic Word. ~Swedenborg, Arcana Coelestia, 6212

From this state, in which I was during the night until morning, I was instructed how the prophets, through whom spirits spake and acted, were possessed; namely, that the spirits had possession of their bodies, insomuch that scarcely anything was left except that they knew that they existed. There were certain spirits appointed to this use, who did not desire to obsess men, but merely to enter into the man's bodily affections; and when they entered into these, they entered into all things of the body. The spirits who were usually with me said that I was absent from them while I remained in this state. ~Swedenborg, Arcana Coelestia 6212

The spirits who possessed my body, as formerly the bodies of the prophets, afterward talked with me, and said that at the time they knew no otherwise than that they had life as when in the body, besides saying much more. I was told further that there were also other influxes with the prophets, to enable them to be at their own disposal, and to use their own thought, only that spirits spake with them, for the most part at that time within them; but that this influx was not into the thought and the will, but was merely a discourse that came to their hearing. ~Swedenborg, Arcana Coelestia 6212

Dreams in Sacred Scripture

As regards dreams, it is known that the Lord revealed the arcana of heaven to the prophets, not only by visions, but also by dreams, and that the dreams were as fully representative and significative as the visions, being almost of the same class; and that to others also as well as the prophets things to come were disclosed by dreams; as by the dreams of Joseph, and of those who were in prison with him, and by those of Pharaoh, of Nebuchadnezzar, and others, from which it may be seen that dreams of this kind, equally with visions, flow in from heaven; with this difference, that dreams occur when the corporeal is asleep, and visions when it is not asleep. How prophetic dreams, and such as are found in the Word, flow in, nay, descend from heaven, has been shown me to the life; concerning which I may relate the following particulars, from experience. ~Swedenborg, Arcana Coelestia 1975

In order that I might fully know how dreams flow in, I was put to sleep, and I dreamed that a ship came laden with delicacies and savory food of every kind. The things in the ship were not seen, but were stowed away. Upon the ship stood two armed guards, besides a third who was its captain. The ship passed into a kind of arched dock. So I awoke and thought about the dream. The angelic spirits, who were above in front to the right, then addressed me, and told me that they had introduced this dream; and in order that I might know with certainty that it was from them, I was put into a state as of sleep and at the same time of wakefulness; and they introduced in the same way various things that were pleasant and delightful; for instance, an unknown little animal which was dispersed in a likeness of blackish and shining rays, that darted with marvelous quickness into my left eye. They also presented men and also little children adorned in various ways; and other things besides, with inexpressible pleasantness, about which I also spoke with them. This was done, not once, but many times, and each time I was instructed by them with the living voice. ~Swedenborg, Arcana Coelestia 1977

The angelic spirits who are at the entrance to the paradisal scenes, are they who insinuate such dreams; and to them is also intrusted the duty of watching over certain men when they sleep, lest they should then be infested by evil spirits. They perform this duty with the greatest delight, so that there is rivalry among them as to who shall be present, and they love to affect the man with the enjoyable and delightful things which they see in his affection and genius. They who have become angelic spirits are from those who in the life of the body had delighted and had loved in every way and with the utmost pains, to make the life of others delightful.

The Cerebellum Is Awake in Sleep

When the hearing is opened sufficiently far, there is heard from them, as from a distance, a sweetly modulated sound, as it were of singing. They said that they do not know whence such things, and representatives so beautiful and pleasant, come to them in a moment; but it was said that it was from heaven. They belong to the province of the cerebellum; for, as I have been informed, *the cerebellum is awake in time of sleep, when the cerebrum sleeps*. From this source the men of the Most Ancient Church had their dreams, together with a perception of what they signified; from whom in great part came the representatives and significatives of the ancients, under which were set forth things that are deeply hidden. ~Swedenborg, Arcana Coelestia, 1977

Moreover there are other spirits, who belong to the province of the left side of the chest, by whom they are often interfered with; as well as by others whom they disregard. ~Swedenborg, Arcana Coelestia 1978

After such dreams I have very frequently been permitted to speak with the spirits and angels who had introduced them; and they told what they had introduced, and I what I had seen. But it would be too tedious to relate all my experience of these matters. ~Swedenborg, Arcana Coelestia 1979

What Spirits Speak and Our Dreams

It is worthy of mention that when after waking I related what I had seen in a dream, and this in a long series, certain angelic spirits (not of those spoken of above) then said that what I related wholly coincided, and was identical, with the subjects they had been conversing about, and that there was absolutely no difference; but still that they were not the very things they had discoursed about, but were representatives of the same things, into which their ideas were thus turned and changed in the world of spirits; for in the world of spirits the ideas of the angels are turned into representatives; and therefore each and all things they had conversed about were so represented in the dream. ~Swedenborg, Arcana Coelestia 1980

They said, further, that the same discourse could be turned into other representatives, nay, into both similar and dissimilar ones, with unlimited variety. The reason they were turned into such as have been described, was that it took place in accordance with the state of the spirits around me, and thus in accordance with my own state at the time. In a word, very many dissimilar dreams might come down and be presented from the same discourse, and thus from one origin; because, as has been said, the things that are in a man's memory and affection are recipient vessels, in which ideas are varied and received representatively in accordance with their variations of form and changes of state. ~Swedenborg, Arcana Coelestia 1980

I may relate one more instance of a similar kind. I dreamed a dream, but a common one. When I awoke, I related it all from beginning to end. The angels said that it coincided exactly with what they had spoken of together; not that the things seen in the dream were the same, for they were wholly different, being things into which the thoughts of their conversation were turned, but in such a way that they were representative and correspondent; and this in every particular, so that nothing was wanting. I then spoke with them about influx, as to how such things flow in and are varied. There was a person of whom I had the idea that he was in natural truth, which idea I had gathered from the acts of his life. ~Swedenborg, Arcana Coelestia 1981

There was a conversation among the angels about natural truth, and on this account that person was represented to me; and the things he said to me, and did, in my dream, followed in order representatively and correspondently from the discourse of the angels with one another. But still there was nothing precisely alike, or the same. ~Swedenborg, Arcana Coelestia 1981

Some souls recently from the world who long to see the glory of the Lord before they are qualified to be admitted, are lulled in regard to the exterior senses and lower faculties in a kind of sweet sleep, and then their interior senses and faculties are aroused into a high degree of wakefulness, and thereby they are admitted into the glory of heaven, but when wakefulness is restored to their exterior senses and faculties, they return into their former state. ~Swedenborg, Arcana Coelestia 1982

Evil Spirits Desire to Attack the Dreamer

Evil spirits most vehemently desire and burn to infest and attack man when he is sleeping, but man is then especially guarded by the Lord, for love does not sleep. The spirits who infest are miserably punished. I have heard their punishments oftener than I can tell; they consist in rendings (spoken of, n. 829, 957, 959), under the heel of the left foot, and this sometimes for hours together. Sirens, who are interior enchantresses, are they who are especially insidious in the night time, and then try to insinuate themselves into a man's interior thoughts and affections, but are as often driven away by the Lord by means of angels, and are at last deterred by the severest punishments. They have also spoken with others in the night time, exactly as if they spoke from me, and as it were with my speech, so like that it could not be distinguished, pouring in filthy things, and persuading false ones. (Swedenborg, Arcana Coelestia, 1983)

The Crew of Sirens

I was once in a very sweet sleep, in which I had nothing but soft repose. When I awoke, some good spirits began to chide me for having (as they said) infested them so atrociously that they supposed they were in hell- throwing the blame upon me. I answered them that I knew nothing whatever about the matter, but had been sleeping most quietly, so that by no possibility could I have been troublesome to them. Astonished at this, they at last had a perception that it had been done by the magic arts of sirens. The like was also shown afterwards, in order that I might know the quality of the crew of sirens. (Swedenborg, Arcana Coelestia, 1983)

They are chiefly of the female sex, who in the life of the body had studied to allure male companions to themselves by interior artifices; insinuating themselves by means of outward things, captivating their lower minds in every possible way, entering into each one's affections and delights, but with an evil end, especially that of exercising command. Hence they have such a nature in the other life that they seem able of themselves to do all things, imbibing and inventing various arts, which they absorb as easily as sponges do waters, whether clean or filthy.

So do they imbibe and put into act things profane as well as holy, with the end, as before said, of exercising command. It has been granted me to perceive their interiors, and to see how foul they are, being defiled by adulteries and hatreds. It has also been granted me to perceive how powerful in its effects is their sphere. They reduce their interiors into a state of persuasion, in order that these may conspire with their exteriors toward such things as they intend. They thus compel and violently draw spirits to think exactly as they do. (Swedenborg, Arcana Coelestia, 1983)

No reasonings appear in connection with them, but they make use of a kind of simultaneous rush of reasonings that are breathed into the person's evil affections and so they work by applying themselves to the natural inclinations, and thereby they get into the lower minds of others, whom they lead on, and by persuasion either overwhelm or captivate them. They study nothing more than to destroy the conscience, and when it is destroyed they get possession of men's interiors, and even obsess the men, although these are ignorant of it.

At this day there are not as formerly external obsessions, but there are internal ones, by spirits of this class. They who have no conscience have become obsessed in this way. The interiors of their thoughts are insane in a manner not unlike this, but are concealed and veiled over by an external decorum and a pretended honorableness, for the sake of their own honor, gain, and reputation. And this such men may know, if they pay attention to their thoughts. ~Swedenborg, Arcana Coelestia 1983

There are three kinds of dreams. The first kind come from the Lord mediately through heaven; such were the prophetic dreams that are treated of in the Word. The second kind come through angelic spirits, especially those who are in front above at the right, where there are paradisal scenes; from this source the men of the Most Ancient Church had their dreams, which were instructive (see n. 1122). The third kind come through the spirits who are near when man is sleeping, which are likewise significative. But fantastic dreams come from a different source. ~Swedenborg, Arcana Coelestia 1976

To make me fully aware of the way that dreams flow in I was put to sleep and dreamt of a boat approaching that was laden with delicacies and savories of every kind. These were stowed away in the boat, out of sight. On deck stood two armed guards, as well as a third man who was the captain. The boat was passing by into a kind of arched dock; and with this I woke up and thought about the dream. At that point the angelic spirits in front and above me over to the right addressed me. They declared that they were the source of this dream. So that I would know for sure that they were the source of it I was brought into a state where I was so to speak both asleep and awake at one and the same time. In a similar way they introduced different things that were pleasing and delightful, for example, an unknown tiny creature which was transformed into an object with blackish and shining rays which shot into my left eye at a fantastic speed. They also presented human beings, and also small children variously adorned, and other things besides whose delightfulness was indescribable. I spoke to those angelic spirits about these things also. This took place not just once but on a number of occasions, and each time they taught me by word of mouth. ~Swedenborg, Arcana Coelestia 1977

Those in whom such dreams originate are angelic spirits at the entrance to the paradise gardens. They are commissioned also to keep watch over certain people who are asleep, to prevent them being molested during that time by evil spirits. They perform their task with very great delight, so much so that they vie with one another to be there, and they love to fill man with joys and delights such as they see within his affection and disposition. Those who have become angelic spirits are drawn from those who during their lifetime took delight in and loved in every way to make other people's lives delightful. ~Swedenborg, Arcana Coelestia 1977

When a person's hearing has been opened far enough he hears as from afar a sweet rhythmic sound like singing coming from these spirits. They declared that they did not know from where such things as these, and representatives so beautiful and delightful, came to them all in a moment; but they were told that they came from heaven. They belong to the province of the cerebellum, for the cerebellum, as I have learned, remains awake even during periods of sleep when the cerebrum is sleeping. This was the **source of the dreams**, *together with the perception of what these meant, which members of the Most Ancient Church had. And from those people were derived most of the representatives and meaningful signs of the Ancients, beneath which things deeply hidden were manifested ~Swedenborg, Arcana Coelestia 1977*

This past night I also observed that there were spirits who presented dreams, and that their life was dreams, while a person is sleeping. When several persons are dreamt of, each spirit plays the role of one person - a fact that I openly discovered upon awakening, for then I spoke quite a while with those who were acting the part of this or that person. The evil spirits' fantasies are foreboding and cruel, as they delight in treating people cruelly. So that I would realize this, their savageness continued for a long time after I awoke, and they could not desist from it. ~Swedenborg, Spiritual Experiences 180

When I had woken up, I thought about the dream, and then I began to speak with those who introduced dreams. They were above me a little to the front, and were speaking, saying that they introduced dreams, but I saw that it was done through them by angelic spirits round about that region where pleasure gardens appear. In order to prove it they even showed me many things while I was awake that they were introducing to others, namely to spirits who were sleeping, with whom I later spoke, and they acknowledged it. ~Swedenborg, Spiritual Experiences 3381

Then I saw the things they introduced, and they were most delightful and of much variety, both things of inexpressible loveliness and also people, little children, adorned in ways that evade all description. In addition to these, I saw at the beginning some unknown tiny animal, which was dispersed like blackening rays that wonderfully spread around the left eye; besides other things I do not remember. ~Swedenborg, Spiritual Experiences 3381

The spirits bringing on the dreams had a kind of loud sound, such as would be that of songs ending faintly in a similar sound. They also said that they could bring on dreams whensoever they wished, which, I suppose, they also did. ~Swedenborg, Spiritual Experiences 3381

About the dreams of spirits. I awoke in a dream, and there appeared to me one spirit who kept on with the dream. From this I was able to learn the state of spirits in dreams, which is not really different from man's, for the still remaining outward and bodily elements in a spirit quiet down like the bodily elements in us do in sleep. I saw this plainly, for he could not fix his attention upon anything except what was going on at the time in his mind. He was speaking, as though not knowing that he spoke. His outer elements were sleeping, his inner ones thus [active] in the dream. 1748, 7 February. !Swedenborg, Spiritual Experiences 664

As for dreams in particular, I would like to say this, that they are brought upon a person by spirits. Dreams by which future events, as well as truths, are revealed, are brought on by spirits of God the Messiah, but the rest by spirits who are not of God the Messiah. But dreams by which people are deceived are caused by evil spirits, thus by the devil's gang. ~Swedenborg, Spiritual Experiences 43

Furthermore, dreams are brought on either by means of actual voices, or for the most part by displays in their countless forms. One who is not acquainted with these can never learn the meaning of symbolic dreams. For the portrayals of realities in heaven are effected by means of the same sort of things as there are on earth, especially those which are gazed upon, thus objects of nature. Sometimes they are composed in such a way that they can hardly be unraveled unless one is acquainted with the individual types of displays. ~Swedenborg, Spiritual Experiences 43

That dreams are of this nature appears very clearly from the dreams of Joseph, as well as of the Pharaoh, and notably those in the books of the prophets, where much is read about dreams. This is not to mention actual visions when people are awake. These visions are also altogether like dreams, being the same kind of displays, just like real life, as if in clear daylight, also at times of wakefulness before and after sleep, as well as other times [see 15]. There are likewise actual portrayals, when the spirits are presented in person just as one person would be to another on earth; but this happened to me when I was in a different state. ~Swedenborg, Spiritual Experiences 43

With some, the dreams brought on by spirits are only illusions amounting to almost nothing but games. They seize upon whatever is brought to mind by the blood and by thoughts that have slipped by, ~Swedenborg, Spiritual Experiences 43

About dreams, how and by whom they are produced. By much experience I have been taught how dreams are produced, and which spirits produce them. I was in a wakeful state, and another was in a state of sleep, or asleep. I was then a spirit so to speak with spirits, and so I was allowed to be among those spirits who introduce dreams, and I also was allowed to introduce dreams, and that this was so I learned from experience, for the other woke up three or four times after the dreams introduced by me, and then I told them, and they were acknowledged. The ones I was allowed to introduce were lovely and pleasant. ~Swedenborg, Spiritual Experiences 3179

Then I was instructed by actual experience who those were who introduced dreams, and how. It was done by symbolic displays intended to delight the sleeper, and they are the ones whose duty it is to keep watch over mankind lest they be attacked by evil spirits while sleeping. This duty they carry out while awake, with the greatest enjoyment, so that there is rivalry as to who of them may be present. And because they are good spirits, they love those dreams that are most pleasant and delightful to [the sleeper]. ~Swedenborg, Spiritual Experiences 3181

On dreams. Moreover there was another who had thought evilly of me in bodily life (which I noticed because he had been speaking about it), even to the point of persecuting me, if permitted, to death. He was also determined to do so, and it was discovered that he would have killed me. That man was also dreaming, and his dream was then displayed to me, by which I discovered something about how he had been, and had attempted intercourse with a virgin in an outhouse. So indeed can those things be uncovered that people had done in the life of the body, manifestly as to all circumstances concerning places and persons. ~Swedenborg, Spiritual Experiences 3383

As regards dreams, it is known that the Lord revealed the arcana of heaven to the prophets, not only by visions, but also by dreams, and that the dreams were as fully representative and significative as the visions, being almost of the same class; and that to others also as well as the prophets things to come were disclosed by dreams; as by the dreams of Joseph, and of those who were in prison with him, and by those of Pharaoh, of Nebuchadnezzar, and others, from which it may be seen that dreams of this kind, equally with visions, flow in from heaven; with this difference, that dreams occur when the corporeal is asleep, and visions when it is not asleep. How prophetic dreams, and such as are found in the Word, flow in, nay, descend from heaven, has been shown me to the life; concerning which I may relate the following particulars, from experience. ~Swedenborg, Arcana Coelestia 1975

There are three kinds of dreams. The first kind come from the Lord mediately through heaven; such were the prophetic dreams that are treated of in the Word. The second kind come through angelic spirits, especially those who are in front above at the right, where there are paradisal scenes; from this source the men of the Most Ancient Church had their dreams, which were instructive (see n. 1122). The third kind come through the spirits who are near when man is sleeping, which are likewise significative. But fantastic dreams come from a different source. ~Swedenborg, Arcana Coelestia 1976

In order that I might fully know how dreams flow in, I was put to sleep, and I dreamed that a ship came laden with delicacies and savory food of every kind. The things in the ship were not seen, but were stowed away. Upon the ship stood two armed guards, besides a third who was its captain. The ship passed into a kind of arched dock. So I awoke and thought about the dream. The angelic spirits, who were above in front to the right, then addressed me, and told me that they had introduced this dream; and in order that I might know with certainty that it was from them, I was put into a state as of sleep and at the same time of wakefulness; and they introduced in the same way various things that were pleasant and delightful; for instance, an unknown little animal which was dispersed in a likeness of blackish and shining rays, that darted with marvelous quickness into my left eye. They also presented men and also little children adorned in various ways; and other things besides, with inexpressible pleasantness, about which I also spoke with them. This was done, not once, but many times, and each time I was instructed by them with the living voice. ~Swedenborg, Arcana Coelestia 1977

The angelic spirits who are at the entrance to the paradisal scenes, are they who insinuate such dreams; and to them is also intrusted the duty of watching over certain men when they sleep, lest they should then be infested by evil spirits. They perform this duty with the greatest delight, so that there is rivalry among them as to who shall be present, and they love to affect the man with the enjoyable and delightful things which they see in his affection and genius. They who have become angelic spirits are from those who in the life of the body had delighted and had loved in every way and with the utmost pains, to make the life of others delightful. When the hearing is opened sufficiently far, there is heard from them, as from a distance, a sweetly modulated sound, as it were of singing. They said that they do not know whence such things, and representatives so beautiful and pleasant, come to them in a moment; but it was said that it was from heaven. ~Swedenborg, Arcana Coelestia 1977

They belong to the province of the cerebellum; for, as I have been informed, the cerebellum is awake in time of sleep, when the cerebrum sleeps. From this source the men of the Most Ancient Church had their dreams, together with a perception of what they signified; from whom in great part came the representatives and significatives of the ancients, under which were set forth things that are deeply hidden. ~Swedenborg, Arcana Coelestia 1977

Moreover there are other spirits, who belong to the province of the left side of the chest, by whom they are often interfered with; as well as by others whom they disregard. ~Swedenborg, Arcana Coelestia 1978

After such dreams I have very frequently been permitted to speak with the spirits and angels who had introduced them; and they told what they had introduced, and I what I had seen. But it would be too tedious to relate all my experience of these matters. ~Swedenborg, Arcana Coelestia 1979

It is worthy of mention that when after waking I related what I had seen in a dream, and this in a long series, certain angelic spirits (not of those spoken of above) then said that what I related wholly coincided, and was identical, with the subjects they had been conversing about, and that there was absolutely no difference; but still that they were not the very things they had discoursed about, but were representatives of the same things, into which their ideas were thus turned and changed in the world of spirits; for in the world of spirits the ideas of the angels are turned into representatives; and therefore each and all things they had conversed about were so represented in the dream. They said, further, that the same discourse could be turned into other representatives, nay, into both similar and dissimilar ones, with unlimited variety. ~Swedenborg, Arcana Coelestia 1980

The reason they were turned into such as have been described, was that it took place in accordance with the state of the spirits around me, and thus in accordance with my own state at the time. In a word, very many dissimilar dreams might come down and be presented from the same discourse, and thus from one origin; because, as has been said, the things that are in a man's memory and affection are recipient vessels, in which ideas are varied and received representatively in accordance with their variations of form and changes of state. ~Swedenborg, Arcana Coelestia 1980

I may relate one more instance of a similar kind. I dreamed a dream, but a common one. When I awoke, I related it all from beginning to end. The angels said that it coincided exactly with what they had spoken of together; not that the things seen in the dream were the same, for they were wholly different, being things into which the thoughts of their conversation were turned, but in such a way that they were representative and correspondent; and this in every particular, so that nothing was wanting. I then spoke with them about influx, as to how such things flow in and are varied. ~Swedenborg, Arcana Coelestia 1981

There was a person of whom I had the idea that he was in natural truth, which idea I had gathered from the acts of his life. There was a conversation among the angels about natural truth, and on this account that person was represented to me; and the things he said to me, and did, in my dream, followed in order representatively and correspondently from the discourse of the angels with one another. But still there was nothing precisely alike, or the same. ~Swedenborg, Arcana Coelestia 1981

Some souls recently from the world who long to see the glory of the Lord before they are qualified to be admitted, are lulled in regard to the exterior senses and lower faculties in a kind of sweet sleep, and then their interior senses and faculties are aroused into a high degree of wakefulness, and thereby they are admitted into the glory of heaven, but when wakefulness is restored to their exterior senses and faculties, they return into their former state. ~Swedenborg, Arcana Coelestia 1982

The Attack of Evil spirits

Evil spirits most vehemently desire and burn to infest and attack man when he is sleeping, but man is then especially guarded by the Lord, for love does not sleep. The spirits who infest are miserably punished. I have heard their punishments oftener than I can tell; they consist in rendings (spoken of, n. 829, 957, 959), under the heel of the left foot, and this sometimes for hours together. Sirens, who are interior enchantresses, are they who are especially insidious in the night time, and then try to insinuate themselves into a man's interior thoughts and affections, but are as often driven away by the Lord by means of angels, and are at last deterred by the severest punishments. They have also spoken with others in the night time, exactly as if they spoke from me, and as it were with my speech, so like that it could not be distinguished, pouring in filthy things, and persuading false ones. ~Swedenborg, Arcana Coelestia 1983

The Crew of Sirens

I was once in a very sweet sleep, in which I had nothing but soft repose. When I awoke, some good spirits began to chide me for having (as they said) infested them so atrociously that they supposed they were in hell-

throwing the blame upon me. I answered them that I knew nothing whatever about the matter, but had been sleeping most quietly, so that by no possibility could I have been troublesome to them. Astonished at this, they at last had a perception that it had been done by the magic arts of sirens. The like was also shown afterwards, in order that I might know the quality of the crew of sirens. ~Swedenborg, Arcana Coelestia 1983

They are chiefly of the female sex, who in the life of the body had studied to allure male companions to themselves by interior artifices; insinuating themselves by means of outward things, captivating their lower minds in every possible way, entering into each one's affections and delights, but with an evil end, especially that of exercising command. Hence they have such a nature in the other life that they seem able of themselves to do all things, imbibing and inventing various arts, which they absorb as easily as sponges do waters, whether clean or filthy.

So do they imbibe and put into act things profane as well as holy, with the end, as before said, of exercising command. It has been granted me to perceive their interiors, and to see how foul they are, being defiled by adulteries and hatreds. It has also been granted me to perceive how powerful in its effects is their sphere. They reduce their interiors into a state of persuasion, in order that these may conspire with their exteriors toward such things as they intend. They thus compel and violently draw spirits to think exactly as they do. ~Swedenborg, Arcana Coelestia 1983

No reasonings appear in connection with them, but they make use of a kind of simultaneous rush of reasonings that are breathed into the person's evil affections and so they work by applying themselves to the natural inclinations, and thereby they get into the lower minds of others, whom they lead on, and by persuasion either overwhelm or captivate them. They study nothing more than to destroy the conscience, and when it is destroyed they get possession of men's interiors, and even obsess the men, although these are ignorant of it. At this day there are not as formerly external obsessions, but there are internal ones, by spirits of this class. They who have no conscience have become obsessed in this way. The interiors of their thoughts are insane in a manner not unlike this, but are concealed and veiled over by an external decorum and a pretended honorableness, for the sake of their own honor, gain, and reputation. And this such men may know, if they pay attention to their thoughts. ~Swedenborg, Arcana Coelestia, AC 1983

Angels With Us

As regards the [telepathic] *influx of angels with a man* [those still living on earth], *it is not an influx of such thoughts as the man then has, but is according to correspondences; for the angels are thinking spiritually, whereas the man perceives this naturally; thus with the man the spiritual things fall into their correspondents, consequently into their* [natural] *representatives.*

For example, when a man speaks of bread, of seedtime, of harvest, of fatness, and the like, the thought of the angels [who are at that moment are connected to the person] *is then about the goods of love and of charity; and so forth* [which are their spiritual correspondences].

I once dreamed a common dream, and when I awoke, I related all from beginning to end. The angels said that all things coincided exactly with those which they had spoken of among themselves; not that these were the same as I had dreamed, but things corresponding and representative, and it is the same in every single thing.

I afterward talked with them about influx [telepathic connection and communication]. *Objects, however, such as a man sees with his eyes, do not appear before the spirits* [those who are in the afterlife] *who are with the man* [people still on earth], *neither are words heard such as the man hears with the ear, but such as the man is thinking.*

That thought is wholly different from speech, is evident from the fact that man thinks in a moment more than he can utter in half an hour, because he thinks abstractedly from the words of language. From this may in some measure be known the nature of the interaction of the soul with the body, namely, that it is such as is the influx of the spiritual world into the natural world; for the soul or spirit of man is in the spiritual world, and his body is in the natural world: thus it is according to correspondences. . ~Swedenborg, Arcana Coelestia, AC 6319

Note the important explanation about those in the afterlife (spirits and angels) who are telepathically connected (influx) to a particular individual on earth. This connection is representative and correspondential, _not direct._ The connections between spiritual things and natural things are never direct but get "translated" or "transformed" into the appropriate representations of each other.

This is important psychologically because it signals the warning that people who claim to hear the voices of God or spirits with their physical ears, or to see ghosts with their physical eyes, are reporting something distinctly abnormal from the perspective of psychopathology.

On the other hand, our normal adaptive everyday thinking (on earth) is made up of natural representatives or images of the spiritual ideas that the spirits who are connected to us are thinking and discussing with each other.

It is awesome to contemplate that God is directly managing these hundreds of connections and disconnections every hour for every human being that has ever been born and this to eternity. What an immense involvement with the human race does this task represent for God!

Think of all the thoughts that come into your mind and succeed each other all day, rivers of thoughts endlessly flowing. Every one of those thoughts is produced in your mind through what the spirits are thinking and discussing. But as soon as your loves and intentions change in the next moment, different thoughts suddenly come into your awareness. These new thoughts are produced by God who is changing the society of spirits to which you are now connected.

These connection patterns with our "vertical community" would be meaningless and useless if the connections were random or did not follow a plan of progression towards a definitive goal for each individual.

Jacob's Ladder

It is evident that God directs all dreams and that this is done by means of telepathic communication with particular spirits and spirit societies in the afterlife. But despite the fact that God so closely manages our thoughts and emotions nevertheless He takes care that we retain our freedom without fail.

After all, consider this: *Where do your thoughts come from?* No one seems to know the answer. But Swedenborg's work demonstrates that thoughts come from, not the individual who has them, but other individuals to whom God connects the person in order to produce the thoughts and feelings that will allow that individual to regenerate. If for instance we become aware of negative thoughts about others or ourselves, we have the opportunity to reject those thoughts and intentions because they are contrary to God and to regeneration.

The process of our regeneration requires that we progress through intermediate steps when transforming our natural-rational consciousness into spiritual-rational consciousness. This transformation is required prior to death so that in the afterlife our personality is equipped with traits that can exist and thrive in the heavenly layers of the human mind.

In the Old Testament we read the well know story of Jacob having a dream of a ladder that reached into heaven and of angels walking up and down while God was standing at the top and looking down on them. Swedenborg's analysis of this dream explains that it represents the process of regeneration on earth whereby our natural-rational thinking is replaced with spiritual-rational thinking. This distinct transformation is called "rebirth" or "being born again".

The angels are said to ascend and descend (not the other way). This is to represent the fact that we need to "ascend" in level of consciousness, and afterward, we need to "descend" back into natural consciousness. This is the healing of wholeness. Our personality in natural consciousness is rearranged into the order of spiritual ideas such as spiritual love or altruism and spiritual truth or rational theistic thinking. Our natural thinking and doing in daily life now corresponds to and represents spiritual good and truth.

The steps of the ladder represent various mental states that we must experience in a certain progressive order. Each step or change in mental state brings us closer to God. We need to remember this! We may observe other people thinking and behaving selfishly or for personal gain. But we are not to condemn others or feel disdain for their life conditions and situations. We are to remember that every step of the ladder is managed and made available by God. We must honor that spiritual fact. There may have to be intermediate steps of goodness and truth that allow the person to move closer to the end. Later these intermediate steps are eliminated and transformed into something more genuinely good.

For instance, it is a general spiritual rule that at every layer of organic operation, interior things are more perfect and closer to God than external things. Consider why people learn new things. There is a sequence of stages involved and each may be considered a wrung on the ladder of raising consciousness. At children we learn for external rewards but later we learn for various other reasons as shown by this progression:

Affection for learning for the sake of
- praise
- reward
- interest
- usefulness to others
- developing our spiritual-rational consciousness
- obedience to God
- love of good and truth, hence love of God

With each step our motivation for learning grows more and more interior and spiritual. To learn fro praise and rewards is relatively external. It involves our surface personality only. If the rewards or praises stop, we lose interest in learning. But later stages are more personal and interior. We learn because we are interested in the topic, and this is more interior. Then we learn things because we realize we can be more useful to others and to society when we know things and have skills. At last we learn new things because we are obedient to God and love good and truth, since this is loving God.

The idea of God is the highest of all human ideas and is biologically implanted in every human soul and mind. Hence when we do something to be obedient to God or God's good and truth, we are operating the highest and deepest motivation in our human personality.

Visions

As regards the first, namely, being withdrawn from the body, the case is this. The man is brought into a certain state that is midway between sleep and wakefulness, and when he is in this state he cannot know but that he is wholly awake. All his senses are as fully awake as in the highest wakefulness of the body; the sight, the hearing, and, wonderful to say, the touch, which is then more exquisite than it can ever be in the wakefulness of the body. In this state also spirits and angels have been seen to the very life, and also heard, and, wonderful to say, have been touched, and almost nothing of the body then intervened. This is the state of which it is said that they are "withdrawn from the body," and that they "do not know whether they are in the body or out of it." 1883-1 I have been let into this state only three or four times, merely that I might know how the case is with it, and that spirits and angels are in the enjoyment of every sense, even touch in a form more delicate and more exquisite than that of the body. ~Swedenborg, Heavenly Secrets, AC 1883

As regards the other kind of vision-being carried away by the spirit into another place-it has been shown me by living experience what it is, and how it is done, but only two or three times. One single experience I may mention. Walking through the streets of a city and through the country, and being at the same time also in conversation with spirits, I did not know but that I was wide awake and saw as at other times, so that I walked on without mistake, and all the time being in vision, seeing groves, rivers, palaces, houses, men, and many other things. But after I had thus walked for hours, suddenly I was in the sight of the body, and became aware that I was in another place. Greatly amazed at this, I perceived that I had been in such a state as they were in of whom it is said that they were "led away by the spirit into another place;" 1884-1 for while this state lasts there is no reflection concerning the way, even if it be many miles; nor is there reflection concerning the time, even if it be many hours or days; nor is there any feeling of fatigue. Moreover the person is led through ways of which he has no knowledge, even to the appointed place. This took place that I might know that a man can be led by the Lord without his knowing whence and whither. ~Swedenborg, Heavenly Secrets, AC 1884

These two kinds of visions, however, are extraordinary, and were shown me merely to the end that I might know their nature. But the things I have habitually "seen" [as mentioned in the title to this work] are all those which of the Lord's Divine mercy you may see related in this First Part, and which are placed at the beginning and end of the several chapters. These are not visions, but things seen in the highest wakefulness of the body, and this for several years. ~Swedenborg, Heavenly Secrets, AC 1885

END OF CHAPTER 4

God, Immortality and Theistic Psychology Series
by Dr. Leon James

© 2016 Leon James and Diane Nahl

http://www.theisticpsychology.org

BOOKS

Jung and Swedenborg on God and Life After Death (2015) (Print and Digital)

Reality is Spiritual Volume 1 Dreams and the Spiritual World Integrating the Psychology of Jung and Swedenborg (current book)

Reality is Spiritual Volume 2 Rational Theistic Self-Analysis (RTS) For Achieving Wholeness Here and in the Afterlife (forthcoming 2016)

Experiencing Regeneration: Equipping Our Personality For Living In The Afterlife (2015) (Print and Digital)

The Conjoined Pair: Natural and Spiritual Marriage (2012) (Print and Digital)

A Man of the Field: Forming the New Church Mind in Today's World (3 Volumes) (2014) (Print and Kindle)

WEB DOCUMENTS

The Correspondential Sense of Sacred Scriptures: Proving that there is a Unified Theistic Psychology Hidden within the World's Historical Sacred Writings (2009)
On the web: http://www.theisticpsychology.org/books/ssss.htm

Best Friends in Love and Together Forever: The Natural and Spiritual Dimension of Marriage (2008)
On the web: http://theisticpsychology.org/books/best-friends-in-love.htm

Principles of Theistic Psychology: The Scientific Knowledge of God Extracted from the Correspondential Sense of Sacred Scripture (18 Volumes) (2004-2008)
On the web:
http://theisticpsychology.org/books/theistic/index.htm

Moses, Paul, and Swedenborg: Three Steps in Rational Spirituality (1999)   http://theisticpsychology.org/books/rationality/moses.html

Swedenborg Encyclopedia of Theistic Psychology: The Ideas of Emanuel Swedenborg (1668-1772) Expressed In Modern Scientific Psychology (1995-2010) (multiple Volumes)
http://theisticpsychology.org/gloss.html

END OF VOLUME 1